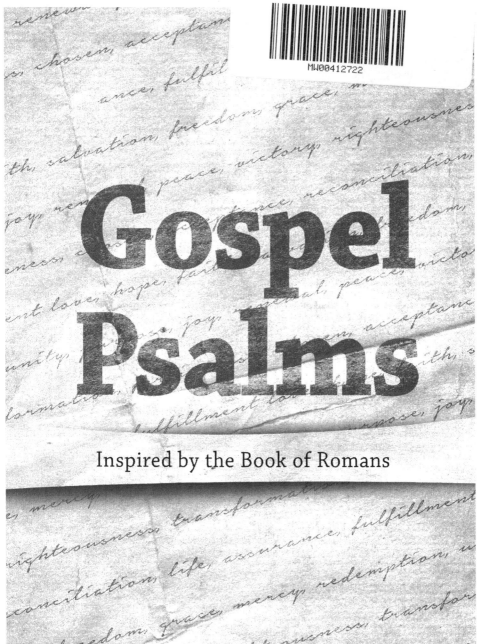

Gospel Psalms

Inspired by the Book of Romans

RON ROWLAND

ISBN-13: 978-1546475903
ISBN-10: 1546475907

CreateSpace Independent Publishing Platform

Cover by Diana Bogardus

Printed in the United States of America

To Sam and Becca

Who inspire me to be my best me

Contents

Preface

Overview

Gospel Psalms is inspired by the book of Romans. It is a series of poems that explore the nature of the good news that God has given us. It is organized into three sections. The first section describes the good news of salvation from the wrath (judgment) of God. It describes everything God has done to save us and the spiritual transformation we have experienced.

The second section of *Gospel Psalms* is called the "Good Life." This section describes the new life that is available to us after we have been saved. This new life is not dependent on circumstances, such as our health or wealth. It does not depend on who we marry or how our children behave. The single factor determining how much of that good life we experience depends on the extent to which we follow the guidance for living that God has provided in his word.

The third section is called "The Goodness of God." These poems describe the character of God, based on passages found in the book of Romans, with respect to such attributes as his righteousness, love, and mercy. As we better understand and more fully experience God's goodness, we want to give God all thanks and all praise.

Format

Gospel Psalms draws its content from the book of Romans, but its format is inspired by the poetry used in the book of Psalms. This poetic format allows for concise statements of biblical truth using illustrations and metaphors. By comparison to a scholarly commentary, *Gospel Psalms* is like the artist's rendering of a house versus an engineer's drawing. Both depict the same house, but the engineer's method emphasizes the accuracy of the dimensions, while the artist attempts to convey its essence.

The poetic format is a means for the truth of God's word both to be understood by the mind and to be felt by the heart. Our understanding of the gospel should not be purely intellectual but also emotional.

Perspective

Gospel Psalms is written from the perspective of one who has been saved by God's grace. That is, it is written by a Christian describing the life and experiences of a Christian. However, the book is not the author's personal journal. Rather, it is intended to reflect experiences, values, and responses common to all Christians. That is why the poems extensively use the pronouns "we," "our," and "us."

Audiences

Gospel Psalms has two intended audiences. It is written to Christians, to help them better understand the full implications of the gospel they have accepted. As they understand just how good the "good news" is, their appreciation of God's love will deepen, and their thankfulness to God for what he has done will be greater. Better understanding the nature of our salvation will help believers to more fully experience in their lives the spiritual changes that have occurred.

The second audience for *Gospel Psalms* is those who are seeking God and the salvation he offers to all, for God uses his love and kindness to draw people to himself. As readers realize the goodness of God and see the benefits of salvation that they are currently missing, it is my prayer they will accept Jesus as their Savior.

Purposes

This book is intended to serve several purposes. One of those purposes is an explanation of biblical doctrine. Poetry is not typically considered a teaching platform, yet the book of Psalms is a rich reservoir of spiritual instruction. These poems are intended to provide teaching on the meaning of the gospel and its implications for those who have been saved. The poems also include teaching the commands of God as to how we should live and how we should relate to others.

The second purpose is to provide an emotional response to what the gospel means to those who have been saved by God's grace through faith in Jesus. Our response to God's gospel must be more than intellectual concurrence. The gospel message speaks directly to the heart, for it is the greatest love story ever told. The foundation of the gospel is the truth that God has a passionate, unconditional love for us.

The third purpose of *Gospel Psalms* is exhortation. Its poems include a call to action for believers. They encourage us to live in a manner consistent with the changes the gospel has caused in our spiritual condition. Scripture says that those who are saved are new creatures in Christ. God has given us a new nature; he has empowered us to live righteously. This righteous living is not only best for us, but God will use us to be a blessing in the lives of others. However, we must choose to use the power God has given us to reap the blessings.

Section I:

The Good News of Salvation

Section I contains a series of poems that explore the good news of our salvation. An appreciation of how our salvation is "good news" can only be reached by understanding the nature of God and the nature of people, as described in the Bible:

- There is a God who created and rules all things. God is holy and has declared that all who sin will die.

- Humanity has rebelled against their creator. Every person has a sin nature and everyone has sinned. All humanity is under God's wrath.

- God has provided a way for people to be saved from his wrath. That way was accomplished through the death of Jesus Christ, Son of God.

- Jesus accepted the punishment for all the sins of all people for all time, thereby allowing God's wrath to be satisfied.

- Anyone can access that salvation by faith in Jesus. All who have placed their trust in Jesus will be saved.

- All who have been saved by faith will live forever in heaven, in the presence of God.

- In heaven, there will be no death or suffering. Our eternity will be filled with peace, joy, love, and fulfillment.

The poems in Section I are divided into three chapters.

- Chapter 1 addresses the actions that God did to secure our salvation.

- Chapter 2 describes the spiritual transformation in our spiritual nature that has occurred as a result of our salvation.

- Chapter 3 describes our new relationship with God that is in effect after we have been saved.

It is certainly possible, if not likely, that we have been saved and yet do not fully understand all that God has accomplished on our behalf. There are a couple of reasons why it is beneficial to fully consider what God has done for us. The first reason is that deeper understanding of the nature of our salvation changes our attitude toward God. God has done far more for us, at a far greater cost than we initially realize.

This understanding causes our love for God to grow deeper, our gratitude to God to increase, and our praise to God to be unending.

The second reason is that as we come to understand the nature of our salvation, we can access its benefits. After we have been saved by faith, we are a new spiritual creature, whether we recognize that or not. We have a new spiritual nature, new powers and abilities, and a new relationship with God.

Once we know the aspects of our new nature, we have a choice. Do we believe what God has declared about us and live accordingly, or do we trust our feelings and perceptions? Here are a couple of examples:

- Do we continue to sin even after we have been saved, believing that we are powerless to resist temptation, or do we believe God, who has declared that we have been set free from the power of sin (Romans 6:6–18)?

- Do we continue to feel guilty for what we have done, or do we believe God, who has said we are no longer under condemnation (Romans 12:1)?

- Do we continue to live as if we are under the obligations of God's law, trying to work our way to heaven, or do we believe God, who has said we are released from the law (Romans 7:4–6)?

Chapter 1:

What God Did to Save Us

The Big Reveal

> *They know the truth about God because he has made it obvious to them… Through everything God made, they can clearly see his invisible qualities—his eternal power and divine nature…*
> *(Romans 1:19-20, NLT)*

Everyone knows there is a God.

God's creation continuously proclaims his existence.

Everywhere we look—everything we hear.

His presence is unmistakable—his existence undeniable

The sky is God's billboard,

continually advertising his presence for all to see.

The earth's bones are an open book,

telling the Creator's story for all to read.

His brushstrokes are seen on every face.

God's law is indelibly written on every heart.

God's existence is self-evident to all humanity,

a truth untouchable, unassailable, undeniable.

We cannot step outside of God's creation—

cannot escape his presence.

The universe reflects its Creator:

- beauty defying description

- complexity exceeding comprehension

- diversity surpassing imagination

- vastness beyond measure

But there was a time when we

- shut our eyes and closed our ears to the truth,
- believed clever lies of our own making,
- shrugged our shoulders at the evidence,
- defiantly turned our backs on our God
- willfully denied the existence of our Creator.

But in his love, God did not

- leave us in a state of denial
- abandon us to hopeless rebellion
- allow us to suffer from his wrath

Even though we did not seek God,
God sought us,
opening our eyes to the truth,
giving us a small kernel of faith
to trust the evidence surrounding us.

Salvation Is Brought to Us

> *For I am not ashamed of the gospel, because it is the power of God that brings salvation to everyone who believes. (Romans 1:6)*

God knew we could not save ourselves.

Those given God's law could not keep it.

Law-teachers were law-breakers.

Those not given the law

had its requirements written on their hearts,

but their actions fell short of their own standards,

doing what they condemned others for doing.

All apart from the law

Will be judged by God

and found guilty

for violating the law of their conscience.

All under the law will be judged by it

and found guilty for their lawless acts.

God knew we could not ascend to heaven,

so he came down to the earth.

God knew we could not pay the penalty for our sin,

so he paid the penalty himself.

God knew we could not keep the law,

so God fulfilled the law in Christ.

God knew we could not save ourselves,

so God sent a Savior.

God brought salvation to us—
the Son of God became the Son of Man.
The ruler of heaven humbly came to the earth.
The righteous one came to sinners.
The light came into the darkness.

Salvation that was once unattainable
has been offered to us.
Salvation that was once out of our grasp
has been brought within our reach.

The gospel
is so unexpectedly simple
that wisdom-seekers are confounded.
The gospel
is so unabashedly humble
that miracle-hunters are disappointed.
And yet we are not ashamed of the gospel,
for only by the gospel
have we been saved.

A Savior Is Sent

> *The gospel he promised beforehand through his prophets in the Holy Scriptures regarding his Son, who as to his earthly life was a descendant of David, and who through the Spirit of holiness was appointed the Son of God in power by his resurrection from the dead: Jesus Christ our Lord. (Romans 1:2–4)*

> *God did by sending his own Son in the likeness of sinful flesh to be a sin offering. (Romans 8:3)*

From the first sin of the first man,
when all of humanity fell under God's wrath,
when our sin separated us from a holy God—
God promised to send a redeemer.
God promised to provide a way of reconciliation.

In hopeful expectation,
the world waited—watching with anticipation,
and God did not disappoint—
God kept his promise.

God sent his Son.
Jesus—the Promised One—the Anointed One,
fulfilling his promise—exceeding expectations.
For God did not just raise up another prophet
to proclaim the word of God
but sent his Son who is the living Word.
God did not just anoint another king
to establish a kingdom on the earth,
but Christ came to establish a heavenly kingdom—
an eternal kingdom where he will reign forever.

Jesus is the Promised One—

- the fulfillment of the ancient prophecies
- the demonstration of God's faithfulness
- the revelation of the hidden mystery
- the embodiment of God's love

Jesus is the living gospel promised by God
who descended from heaven to dwell among us.
Jesus came
to rescue the perishing—deliver the imprisoned.
Jesus came
to redeem the enslaved—find the lost.
Jesus came
to give his life so we might live.

We are thankful for Jesus Christ.
In him,
our hope for a redeemer has been realized.
In him,
God's promise of deliverance has been kept.
In Jesus,
we are saved.

Our Savior Died for Our Sins

> *For all have sinned and fall short of the glory of God. (Romans 3:23)*

> *While we were still sinners, Christ died for us. (Romans 5:8)*

We were sinners.
That was what we did—that was who we were.
We were sinners
in the presence of a holy God
who will not tolerate sin.
We were sinners
in the sight of a just God
who will not allow sin to go unpunished.
We were sinners
by our nature—by our actions—through Adam.

But we were sinners
in the arms of a loving God
who desired that none would perish.
And we were sinners
in view of a gracious God
who gave us what we did not deserve.

Given the nature of God and the nature of man,
there was only one way we could be saved.
God did for us what we could not do for ourselves.
God himself

- accepted the punishment we deserved

- paid the penalty for our sin

- reconciled us to himself

God provided a substitute to be punished in our place.
God sent Jesus Christ to die for our sins.
The sinless man—the Son of God,
the perfect sacrifice on whom
the wrath of God has fallen.

It is the wonderful mystery of the cross that

- Jesus's blood would cover all our sins
- his death would appease the wrath of God
- his sacrifice would satisfy God's perfect justice

God's plan was the perfect solution.
There was justice—every sin was punished.
There was atonement—every penalty was paid.
There was grace—the guilty were pardoned.
There was love—the perishing were saved.

Thank you, Jesus.
You carried the burden of our sin
as you walked to the cross.
You accepted the wrath of God for our sin
as you hung upon the cross.
You exchanged your righteousness for our sin
as you died on that cross.

The death of the Creator
caused a spiritual earthquake through all creation,
sending a tsunami of grace over all humanity,
from the beginning of time—forward to its end.
The death of Jesus
caused a cloud of God's forgiveness
to spread from Jerusalem,
encircling the globe—enveloping all peoples.

Our Savior Rose from the Dead

Christ died and rose again for this very purpose—to be Lord both of the living and of the dead. (Romans 14:9 NLT)

As Jesus was dying on the cross,
the dreams of his followers died with him.
They knew the terrible finality of death.
When his dead body was placed in the tomb,
their last bit of hope disappeared in its darkness.
They knew the dreadful certainty of the grave.

But nothing is final until God declares
it is finished.
No fate is certain unless
it is the will of God,
and God's plan was the resurrection of Jesus.

The resurrection is

- the foundation of the gospel

- the basis for our faith

- the reason for our hope

The resurrection

- proclaims he is the Lord of the living and dead

- demonstrates Jesus's victory over death and sin

- reveals Jesus is the Son of God

- shows God was satisfied with Jesus's sacrifice

- gives us confidence in our future resurrection

Jesus Christ is alive,
leaving behind the evidence of the empty tomb.
No fallen hero—no dead prophet—no buried martyr
but our living Lord.
Jesus reigns in heaven,
our living Savior
who will return to bring us home.

Thank you, Jesus.
As we share in your death,
we will share in your life.
As we share in your resurrection,
we will share in your victory.
The resurrection of our souls
has already happened.
The resurrection of our bodies
is promised but is yet to come.

God Called Us

> *You also are among those Gentiles who are called to belong to Jesus Christ. ⁷ To all in Rome who are loved by God and called to be his holy people. (Romans 1:6–7)*

> *And those he predestined, he also called; those he called, he also justified; those he justified, he also glorified. (Romans 8:30)*

> *For God's gifts and his call are irrevocable. (Romans 11:29)*

We were always the object of God's affection.
Even before creation existed—
before the beginning of time—
God knew us and chose us
to receive his mercy—enjoy his grace.

The mystery of God's choosing is

- shrouded in his omniscience,

- hidden in the eternal,

- beyond our comprehension.

Those who were chosen by God
were called by God,
drawing to himself those who were not seeking him—
saving those who didn't realize they were perishing.

God's call is irresistible,
like moths to a light.
All who are called will answer it,
receiving Jesus as their Savior.
God's call is irrevocable—
a final decree—an unalterable agreement.
All who are called are forever saved.

To those he called, God gave

- life when we were spiritually dead

- sight when we were blind to our sin

- hearing when we were deaf to the gospel

- faith when we trusted only ourselves

Praise to the living God.
Salvation is all by him and not by us.
Absent God's calling

- none of us would seek him

- none of us would respond to the gospel

- none of us would be saved

A Powerful Gospel Is Unleashed

For I am not ashamed of the gospel, because it is the power of God that brings salvation to everyone who believes. (Romans 1:16)

The gospel seems foolish to many,
for it comes with no miracles
other than the miracle of salvation.
The gospel confounds the intellectuals,
for it demands no education—no superior intelligence—
only simple faith in a simple truth.
The gospel upsets the strong—the powerful,
for salvation requires no status,
only the humility to receive a gift.
Those held in highest regard by the world
may have nothing but disdain for the gospel,
for it seems to appeal to the weak—to the poor—
to the powerless.

But we are not ashamed of the gospel,
for it has great power to save
that does not come from within us
but from above.
And we are not ashamed of the gospel,
for we all were poor in spirit—powerless against sin—
weak in righteousness.

The gospel message cannot be denied—
cannot be excluded or ignored,

- penetrating the hardest heart

- attracting the most disinterested

- foiling every attempt to stop its impact

For the gospel is the word of God,

- cutting through every barrier

- speaking directly to our heart

- drawing us to him

The power of the gospel enables us to

- put aside what once seemed urgent

- ignore what once seemed irresistible

- do what once seemed impossible

The power of the gospel transforms lives

- providing hope to the hopeless

- saving the perishing

- giving life to the spiritually dead

The spread of the gospel cannot be stopped
because it is the power of God.
There is no distance too great—no barrier too strong,
no culture so indifferent, no government so hostile
to suppress the good news that Jesus saves.

We take the gospel with us,
wherever we go—whatever we do.
The gospel's power can be displayed

- in every relationship

- in every conversation

- in every location

It is a contagion of good news that cannot be denied.
The spread of the gospel
does not rely upon the power of the messenger
but on the power of message.

Thank you, Lord God,
for the gospel's irresistible attraction—
its unstoppable message.
For if the gospel was any less powerful,
we would not have been saved.

Salvation by Faith

> *This righteousness is given through faith in Jesus Christ to all who believe. ... God presented Christ as a sacrifice of atonement, through the shedding of his blood—to be received by faith. (Romans 3:22, 25)*
>
> *A person is justified by faith apart from the works of the law. (Romans 3:28)*

How can we live in God's holy presence
if we are not perfect in holiness?
How can we obtain the perfect righteousness
God's justice demands?
How can the imperfect ever become perfect—
the sinner ever become sinless?
How can we ever do enough to earn our salvation?
We cannot.

But God did for us
what we could never do for ourselves.
God gave us
what we lacked but could never obtain.
God gave us
the perfect righteousness of Christ,
a righteousness given in grace—received through faith.

Faith in Jesus does not make us righteous,

but faith is the conduit

through which we receive his perfect righteousness.

Faith is like a pipe carrying water

to the thirsty in the desert.

The pipe itself does not quench thirst,

but it supplies the water that does.

Faith in Jesus is the only source of living water

in the desert of sin.

God knew our works would never be sufficient

to bridge the gap

between the terrible wrath of God we deserve

and the salvation he has prepared for us.

In his grace, God provided a bridge of faith

for us to walk upon from darkness to light—

from death to life.

Faith is the only bridge

from earth to heaven.

A narrow bridge—a solitary bridge

that is not discovered by our efforts

but is revealed to us by God himself.

Faith in Jesus is the only way to salvation.

All Who Believe Are Saved

If you declare with your mouth, "Jesus is Lord," and believe in your heart that God raised him from the dead, you will be saved. For it is with your heart that you believe and are justified, and it is with your mouth that you profess your faith and are saved…. "Everyone who calls on the name of the Lord will be saved." (Romans 10:9–10, 13)

God loves all people
and desires that none would perish.
Regardless of what we have done,
regardless of who we are,
God loves us.
The wonder of God's gospel is that
everyone who believes in Jesus will be saved.

God's gospel has no performance prerequisites—
no preconditions, no moral prequalification.
There are no exclusions.
Everyone who believes will be saved.

Faith in Jesus requires nothing.
Anyone can believe, anywhere, anytime.
We don't acquire faith by being worthy.
We don't keep faith by our performance.
There are no language barriers—no prerequisites,
no training to complete, no rituals to perform.

Those saved by God include people
from every tribe, every nation, every generation.
Those who are saved include
the rich and the poor, the young and the old,
the famous, the infamous, the anonymous.

There is only one thing we all have in common —
faith in Jesus.
We thank God for the gift of faith.
Faith allows

- our hardened hearts to be drawn toward him

- our wayward feet to turn back to him

- our spiritual eyes to be opened to the truth

If salvation were based on our merit,
we would not be saved.
If salvation were based on our performance,
we would have no hope.
But by God's grace, we
are saved by faith in Jesus.
He is infinitely worthy.
His righteousness is complete.
His sacrifice was perfect.

Chapter 2:

Our Spiritual Transformation

The Guilty Are Acquitted

> *To show that the entire world is guilty before God. (Romans 3:19 NLT)*
>
> *For all have sinned and fall short of the glory of God, and all are justified freely by his grace through the redemption that came by Christ Jesus. (Romans 3:23–24)*
>
> *God ... declares sinners to be right in his sight when they believe in Jesus. ... our acquittal is not based on obeying the law. It is based on faith. (Romans 3:26–27 NLT)*

There was no doubt we were guilty.
All of us had done what God's law prohibited.
All had failed to do what God's law required.
There was no doubt our sins were known.
An omniscient God had seen all we had done—
knew all our thoughts and motives.

There was no question of the punishment.
God had declared all who sinned would die.
There was no escape
from the wrath of an omnipotent God.

But God our judge is merciful—
acquitting us of all charges.
This is no miscarriage of justice—
no wink and nod by the judge.
With God, there is both mercy and justice.
The punishment was rendered
for all our sins.
The penalty was paid
for all our transgressions—
not by us but by God.

Christ took the punishment on our behalf.
Christ paid the debt we owed.
For the first time in our lives,
we were made right with God

There is relief when the innocent are acquitted—
when the falsely accused are declared not guilty.
But there is incredulous amazement
when the guilty are declared innocent
and are set free.

May we embrace our acquittal
with awestruck acceptance.
God's acquittal

- takes away the burden of guilt

- shields us from attacks by the accuser

- gives us certain hope for the future

We walk with the joy of the condemned
who have been set free.
We will not grow weary of telling
our story of the guilty being acquitted.
We will always have wondering amazement
that Christ would love someone like us—
that Christ would die for someone like me.

The Condemned Are Saved

All who sin apart from the law will also perish apart from the law, and all who sin under the law will be judged by the law. (Romans 2:12)

Since we have now been justified by his blood, how much more shall we be saved from God's wrath through him! (Romans 5:9)

We once stood condemned before God

- by our own conscience
- by the devil's accusations
- by God's law

We deserved God's judgment—
ripe for God's wrath to fall on us

God's wrath did fall—
but not on us.
Jesus chose to take our place.
The full wrath of God fell on him.

- the sinless one took our sin
- the innocent one was punished
- the blameless one was blamed

The righteous wrath of God was satisfied.

God's wrath against our sin did not vanish
but was absorbed by Jesus.
God's wrath was not diluted,
but all of it was poured out on our Savior
for every sin we would ever commit.

No longer do we fear God's judgment,
for now there is no condemnation.
We have been made right with God.
No longer is God our judge but our father,
for he has adopted us into his family.

Praise to Jesus for his love for us—
for his willing obedience to be the perfect sacrifice.
Only his blood could cover all our sins.
Only his perfect righteousness was sufficient.
Only he could save us.

The Unrighteous Are Given Righteousness

There is no one righteous, not even one. (Romans 3:10)

Through the obedience of the one man the many will be made righteous. (Romans 5:19)

Christ is the culmination of the law so that there may be righteousness for everyone who believes. (Romans 10:4)

None of us were righteous—none were perfect.
All of us were flawed by sin.
There was nothing we could ever do
to be right in the sight of God.
We had no glue to fix our shattered lives—
no cleanser to remove sin's indelible stain,
no caulk to fill the cracks in our soul.
What we could not do for ourselves,
God did for us.

God did not leave us as perpetual lawbreakers—
always in the wrong, never right with God.
He gave us a righteousness
apart from our obedience to law.
God sent Jesus—perfect in obedience—
who fulfilled the law for us.

God did not leave us in spiritual poverty,

in moral bankruptcy,

unable to repay our debt of sin.

We had only treasures on earth.

We lacked the righteousness

that is the currency of heaven.

But by God's grace,

the infinite riches of Christ's righteousness

were deposited in our account.

Now we owe nothing but the debt of love.

All our lives had been stained by sin—

a stain we could not remove, could not cover up.

We were unfit for the purity of heaven.

But God did not leave us as we were.

He cleansed us with the blood of Jesus,

making us pure and holy in his sight.

Thank you, God,

for making the imperfect

perfect in Jesus.

For making the unrighteous

righteous in Jesus.

For making the impure

pure through him.

Freed from Sin

> *For we know that our old self was crucified with him so that the body ruled by sin might be done away with, that we should no longer be slaves to sin ... For sin shall no longer be your master, because you are not under the law, but under grace ... though you used to be slaves to sin ... You have been set free from sin and have become slaves to righteousness. (Romans 6:6, 14, 17–18)*

Sin was heroin for our souls.
Our initial dalliance become a craving.
Then its allure filled our thoughts—
overpowered our will.
What we once sought for enjoyment
became our ruthless master.
What we once toyed with
controlled us.

Sin was the tiger within us,
which we fed when it seemed small and harmless.
Sin was the tiger within us
that became strong and fierce and hungry.
We continued to feed it
more and more—for we feared it.

One small sin led to more sins
and greater sins
until we believed that we had no choice
but to sin even more.

Unable to free ourselves from sin's grip,
powerless against sin's addictive appeal,
our condition progressively worsened.
We were sliding down into the pit
with no hope of ever ascending.

But Christ was our deliverer
Who rescued us from sin's captivity.
Christ was our redeemer
who paid our ransom.
We relish the liberty we have in him.
Now we enjoy the freedom to do good.
Now we savor the blessings of life
that God always intended for us.

Only a former slave
can fully savor the taste of liberty.
Only a former addict
can fully appreciate freedom from its grip.
Only those rescued from captivity
can deeply express gratitude to the deliverer.

We are
former slaves of sin
who have been given liberty.
We are
former addicts to sin's desires
who have been set free.
We are
former captives of the lord of darkness
who have been released.

Our old nature died in Christ.
Now we have a new nature
that derives no satisfaction from sin
but rejoices in pleasing God.
A nature with the power to resist temptation
and the desire to do what is right.

God's grace was given
so we would be free from sin,
not free to sin.
Now we live for the glory of God
and the good of others.

May we not be
a prisoner who has been freed
yet chooses to return to prison.
May we not be
one who has received a great inheritance
yet chooses to live in poverty.

We are former sin-prisoners
who now soar in wonder of God's grace.
We are former sin-addicts
who now dance with abandonment in our freedom.

We are dead to sin but alive to God.
No longer instruments of evil but of righteousness,
no longer slaves to sin but children of God,
no longer living for self but living for Jesus.

Freed from the Law

> *You also died to the law through the body of Christ … For when we were in the realm of the flesh, the sinful passions aroused by the law were at work in us, so that we bore fruit for death. But now, by dying to what once bound us, we have been released from the law. (Romans 7:4–6)*

God's law is a holy rain.
It brings life to the righteous,
causing them to bear fruit
pleasing to God.
But none of us were righteous,
so when God's law was revealed—
as the holy rain of his commands fell upon us—
the seeds of sin within us sprouted,
and we bore the fruit of death.

Some rose in angry rebellion to God's law
with a passion to taste what is forbidden,
with a blatant disregard for God's commands,
with a desire to be their own god.

Others rose in zealous striving
to obey God's law,
puffing themselves up with pride
at their accomplishments,
hiding their failures
under the cover of denials.

Whether zealous striving or defiant rebellion,
the law did not make us more righteous—
did not save us.
It only caused the seeds of sin to grow.

Thank you, Jesus.
You have freed us from the law,
fulfilling all its requirements
on our behalf.
You have freed us to serve you in a new way—
the way of the Spirit.

No longer do we obey to avoid punishment,
for God no longer condemns us
but we obey because we are thankful.

No longer do we obey out of fear,
for the wrath of God has been appeased,
but we obey because we are loved.

No longer do we rebel against the law,
for Christ has fulfilled all its requirements,
leaving nothing to rebel against.

No longer are we motivated by pride,
for Christ accomplished everything for us,
leaving no room for boasting.

The way of the Spirit is life.
Guidance has replaced requirements.
Opportunity has replaced obligations.
Anticipation has replaced dread.

Peace with God

Therefore, since we have been justified through faith, we have peace with God through our Lord Jesus Christ. (Romans 5:1)

We rebelled against our Creator.
We went to war against our God.
And God responded
with a relentless wrath against sin.
Every sin had a consequence—
every consequence brought pain.

Our spirits continually contended with God,
but it was a war we could never win.
Who can defeat the Almighty?
What created thing is greater than its Creator?
It is like trying to fight gravity.
Gravity is always there—gravity always wins.

We were unwilling to reconcile with God,
unable to make it right.
We had no peace.
There was no rest.

But now we have peace with God through Jesus.
By his death and resurrection,
he has won the victory—he has ended the conflict.
Christ has reconciled God with man.
He accepted God's wrath against sin on our behalf.
He fulfilled all the law's requirements for us.
He gave us his righteousness in exchange for our sin.

God has given us a new nature.

No longer do our souls wish to contend with God,

for we are one with God.

No longer do we strive to please ourselves,

but desire to please God.

No longer do we wish to battle against God,

for we have unconditionally surrendered.

It is a peace

that is more than cessation of hostilities—

more than an uneasy truce.

God has made us right with him—

God has made us one with him.

He loves us as his children

and we love God as our heavenly Father.

Our peace with God provides

- harmony with our Lord

- oneness with our heavenly Father

- relationship with our Creator

In God's peace

There is no place for anxiety—no reason to worry.

Our restless souls are calmed.

Our weary bodies can rest

in the arms of the Father.

Thank you, Jesus—Prince of Peace.

We sought conflict, but you brought us peace.

We caused separation, but you brought us reconciliation.

We lived in anxiety, but you brought us assurance.

Now we walk in the peace we have been given—

embracing the reconciliation—living with contentment.

The Gift of Eternal Life

> *But now that you have been set free from sin ... the result is eternal life. For the wages of sin is death, but the gift of God is eternal life in Christ Jesus our Lord. (Romans 6:22–23)*

We worked in sin's factory—
harvested crops from sin's farm.
The wages for our labor was death.
That was the destiny we earned—
the judgment we deserved.

But God chose to give us the gift of eternal life.
Eternal life is

- more than escaping death

- more than avoiding the grave

- more than evading punishment

Eternal life is

- fulfilling the purpose for which we were created

- achieving the fullness of joy God intended

- enjoying peace beyond imagination

- resting in the security of our salvation

- experiencing oneness with God himself

We have been privileged to experience
appetizers of the love, peace, and fulfillment
that we will fully enjoy at heaven's feast.

We have been privileged to see
flashes and glimpses of God's glory
as a foretaste of what is to come
surrounding heaven's throne.

When Christ returns and takes us home,
we will be in God's presence forever and ever,
perpetually surrounded by his glory.
Throughout eternity
We will be continually amazed
at the abundance of his grace,
the immeasurable depth of his love.
We will always be filled
with thanks for all that God has done.

When Christ returns and takes us home,

- our mortal bodies become immortal

- suffering disappears into a sea of joy

- frustration gives way to fulfillment

- separation dissolves into union with God

- and the curse is replaced by perpetual blessings

Our hearts are filled with gratitude
for the gift of life God has given us.
Our hearts ache
for those who have not accepted it.
We want everyone we love—everyone we know—
to join us in heaven—to experience eternal life.
It is our prayer that the whole world
Will accept God's gift of eternal life—
will trust in Jesus for their salvation.

Spiritual Resurrection

Just as Christ was raised from the dead through the glory of the Father, we too may live a new life. (Romans 6:4)

Give yourselves completely to God, for you were dead, but now you have new life. (Romans 6:13 NLT)

All have sinned,

and God has said all who sin will die.

It was our certain fate, our inevitable destiny—

death of the body and death of the spirit.

But we tried to ignore the decaying of our bodies.

We tried to deny the inevitable, delay the certain.

We clung to the notion that we were somehow immune

from the fatal sickness that affected all others.

That against all odds,

we would somehow escape

the destiny of all who preceded us.

But undeniable is the power of death.

There is no escape from its reach.

Fallen heroes, nefarious criminals,

the rich and the famous, the poor and the anonymous,

Those beloved by all and those universally hated—

death was our common destiny.

But the only certainty is the plan of God.

The only destiny that endures

is the one written by the finger of God.

And God rewrote our destiny,

for his grace is greater than our sin.

We who were born into spiritual death
were awakened by the kiss of God,
who breathed his Spirit into our souls,
and we were given new life in Christ.

This new life means we have

- a fresh start

- a new beginning

- a clean slate

It is a life with possibilities previously unimagined,
a life with new hopes and dreams.

We are like someone with a failing heart
who received a transplant.
Now we have renewed vigor and energy.
Now we have hope for the future.

We are like refugees who fled
a country filled with war and suffering,
who immigrated to a new land
where they found peace—
where they were blessed with opportunities.

We have new life in Christ.
Godly thoughts have replaced sinful thoughts.
Righteous actions have replaced sinful actions.
We want to please God rather than ourselves.
We ponder what we can do help others
rather than scheming how others can help us.

The life we now live—
planned for us by God himself—
is full of purpose, rich in relationships,
abundant in blessings.

The riches of God's grace
took away our spiritual poverty.
The abundance of his love
filled the emptiness of our souls.
The living water that is Jesus
quenched our thirst for belonging.

In the life we now enjoy

- gratitude has swept away our bitterness

- joy has sprung out of depression

- peace has replaced anxiety

We now enjoy a special sweetness of life
tasted by the rescued who were once perishing.
We now experience a depth of gratitude
felt by the dying who were given life.

No Condemnation by God

> *Therefore, there is now no condemnation for those who are in Christ Jesus, because through Christ Jesus the law of the Spirit who gives life has set you free from the law of sin and death. (Romans 8:1–2)*

God is no longer our judge
who punishes us in righteous anger
but now is our Father
who loves us as his children.

No longer do we try to hide our sin from God
but now confidently turn to him for forgiveness.
No longer do we feel shame
for what we have done—for who we are,
but now we know we are accepted by God.
It is an unalterable, immutable acceptance
guaranteed by the promises of God himself.

We no longer worry
if we are doing enough for God,
but have the assurance
that Christ has fulfilled everything for us.
We no longer fear a pending judgment
but rest in the fact that God has already acquitted us.

Through Christ
we are right with God,
today, tomorrow, forever.
Not because of our actions
but despite our conduct.
Not because of our righteousness
but due to God's grace.

When we sin—even in our new life—
people will rightly accuse us—
our conscience will naturally convict us.
But knowing our salvation is secure
gives us the confidence—gives us the courage
to confess our sin, to ask for forgiveness,
to make restitution.

Knowing we are right with God
means we are not burdened with guilt—
not lurking in the shadows of shame—
but walking in the light of the Father's love
with the confidence that God has already pardoned us.

Adopted into God's Family

> *For those who are led by the Spirit of God are the children of God. ... the Spirit you received brought about your adoption to sonship. ... The Spirit himself testifies with our spirit that we are God's children. (Romans 8:14–16)*

We are children of God.

- not by birth but by adoption
- not by our right but by God's choice
- not by God's obligation but by his love

As adopted children, we are not the lesser
but walk with the assurance of the chosen.
As adopted children, we were not born with rights—
not born with expectations
but have the gratitude of the unwanted
becoming wanted—the joy of the abandoned
who now belongs.

We were born outside of God's family
in spiritual poverty,
but now we are heirs—now we have an inheritance.
From birth our destiny was death,
but now we have been given eternal life.

God is our Father.

No longer do we run away from him in fear

as the judge of our sins.

Now we run toward him with the assurance

that our Father loves us.

No longer do we anxiously search for security.

Now we walk with the assurance that our father

will protect us and provide for us.

Chapter 3:

Our New Relationship with God

The Holy Spirit Intercedes for Us

> *The Spirit helps us in our weakness. We do not know what we ought to pray for, but the Spirit himself intercedes for us through wordless groans. And he who searches our hearts knows the mind of the Spirit, because the Spirit intercedes for God's people in accordance with the will of God. (Romans 8:26–27)*

We know we are to pray,

and we know how to pray,

for we have the example of Jesus,

but we don't always know what to ask

So many times what we thought was best

turned out to be a mistake.

So many times what seemed to be terrible

turned out to be good.

But the Holy Spirit knows the future—

knows what is best for us,

knows God's will for us,

and he intercedes on our behalf

The Holy Spirit does not replace our prayers
but enhances them.
We still need to pray,
for prayer changes us—causing our will
to align with the will of God.

Let us pray with the confidence
that God's response does not depend
on our skill in making the right request
at just the right time

We now pray with the confidence
that the Holy Spirit is interceding for us—
that he is adding to our feeble prayers.
Then they become the prayers
our heart and spirit would want to offer
if they knew what to ask.
Then they become the prayers
aligned with the will of God.
Then they become the prayers
God will answer.

God Works for Our Good

> *And we know that in all things God works for the good of those*
> *who love him, who have been called according to his purpose.*
> *(Romans 8:28)*

The Lord God has made a wonderful promise
to all his children—
to all those chosen and called by God.
His promise is
that he works for our good "in all things."

We believe in the promise
but lack understanding of his ways.
We wonder how can it be good

- when we lose our job and then our home

- when a friend has cancer and is dying

- when we are dying and don't have a friend

For in the darkness of those times,
we do not see—cannot see the good.
But God shows us in his word
how good can result from evil—
how the terrible can become wonderful.

Look at the life of Joseph:

- hated for doing right

- sold into slavery by his own brothers

- taken to a foreign land

- imprisoned due to a false accusation

Could Joseph see the good in that?

But injustice and suffering
were the path to Joseph's rise to power in Egypt—
from prison to the palace
where Joseph was able to save his family.

Even though Joseph's brothers
did intend to harm him,
God intended it for good.
Even though they meant it for evil,
God meant it for good.

Look at the life of Jesus:

- hated by the very people he came to save

- betrayed by one of his chosen disciples

- illegally arrested, unjustly convicted

- wrongfully crucified

How could his disciples see any good in that?

And yet later his disciples understood.
Jesus' death was planned by God—orchestrated by God
to be the necessary sacrifice for our sin.
Jesus' life was not taken but willingly given
to fulfill the purposes of God.

Only God can use the world's evil actions
to work for the good of his chosen.
Only God can use humanity's wicked motivations
to accomplish his holy purposes.

When God speaks of "the good," it means

- his purposes are achieved

- his plan is fulfilled

- his will is accomplished

And we rest in the assurance that
God's good is always our good.

When we are in the middle of pain and suffering,
we often cannot see a good outcome—
we cannot even imagine how good could result.
And yet we can be confident
that good will occur for all who
have faith in God.

We may never see or understand God's purposes
on this side of heaven.
But we have the assurance
that he is always working for our good,
whether we believe it or not.
God's promises
do not rest on our faith but in his faithfulness—
do not rely on our strength but in his power.

God Is for Us

> *If God is for us, who can be against us? He who did not spare his own Son, but gave him up for us all—how will he not also, along with him, graciously give us all things? (Romans 8:31–32)*

We all need a friend

- who will not abandon us in tough times

- who will always be on our side

- who wants what is best for us

For we were not made to walk through life alone.

And if we have no friends—if no one stands with us—
We can rest in this assurance—
God is always for us. He is always with us.
He will not leave us. He will never forsake us.

Knowing God is for us
means it does not matter who is against us.
The words of our critics may sting us,
but we will not be silenced.

The threats of enemies may be heard,
but we will not be intimidated.
The rejection of friends may hurt us,
but we will not be discouraged.

Knowing God is with us enables us
To persevere in suffering—to overcome adversity.
We can trust God to give us everything we need:

- courage in the face of danger

- hope in times of despair

- love in our nights of loneliness

God is like that friend who walks with us
through the dark alleys of life.
God is like the one who bails us out of jail
when all others abandon us.
God is like the one who sits with us
when we wait for death to come.
God is all of that and more.

Victory over Adversity

> *Can anything ever separate us from Christ's love? Does it mean he no longer loves us if we have trouble or calamity, or are persecuted, or hungry, or destitute, or in danger, or threatened with death … No, despite all these things, overwhelming victory is ours through Christ, who loved us. (Romans 8:35, 37 NLT)*

We will have times of trouble and tribulation,
but until our mission for God is completed,
he will deliver us.

We will have times of hardship and deprivation,
but until God's purpose for our life is finished,
he will provide for our needs.

We will face persecution and threats,
but until our work for God on earth is done,
he will protect us.

God's love for us
does not spare us from pain and suffering.
God did not spare his own Son,
who suffered greatly and was killed
for doing the work of the Father.

God's love for us
allows us to not only endure tough times
but to emerge from them victoriously

- with our faith in God strengthened

- with our gratitude to him deepened

- with our hope in his promises unshaken

We will always be victorious in adversity
when our actions are God's will.
Victory does not come from our strength.
The victory is achieved *through him who loved us.*

God will call us home in victory

- when our mission here is complete

- when our work here is done

- and his purposes for us have been achieved

In that heavenly home
there will be no more sin and death—
no more pain and suffering,
where we will be given an immortal body
and live in God's presence forever
thanks to the victory
that has been won by Jesus Christ.

No Separation from God's Love

> *For I am convinced that neither death nor life, neither angels nor demons, neither the present nor the future, nor any powers, neither height nor depth, nor anything else in all creation, will be able to separate us from the love of God that is in Christ Jesus our Lord. (Romans 8:38–39)*

God's love is not like our love,

for it is unbreakable, unending, unconditional.

God's love can never be

- overcome by a greater attraction

- overwhelmed by adversity

- undermined by offensive words or actions

- weakened by distance

- eroded by time

- separated by death

The power of his love always rages

like a mountain stream in the spring.

There is nothing within us

that can extinguish or diminish God's love,

for his love does not depend on our response.

There is nothing outside of us

that is strong enough to break God's loving grasp,

for God has no equal.

God's love is not like our love.
We can never anger God—disappoint God
Such that he no longer loves us.
It is never too late to be loved by God.
We never go too far for God to rescue us.
Nothing can separate us from the love of God.

We are certain of this because of the cross of Jesus.
The cross demonstrates the power of God.
Through Jesus's crucifixion and resurrection,
death and sin were defeated.
The cross demonstrates the extravagant love of God,
for Jesus willingly suffered and died for us
when we were his enemies.

Our great comfort and assurance is this.
God's unfailing love is

- always with us

- always sustaining us

- always protecting us.

His love for us will eternally endure.
Our salvation is forever secure.

Section II:

The Good Life

We all want to enjoy the "good life." God wants us to have that as well. Unfortunately, the way we think we can achieve it is often quite different than God's way. Our view often equates the good life with favorable circumstances. That is, we are experiencing the good life when we have:

- money or possessions;

- fame, power, or status;

- freedom to indulge in whatever we want;

- family and friends who respect and love us; or

- a healthy body.

However, none of the above is guaranteed to us. Even if we experience some aspects of the good life for a season, it does not endure. Money is spent; possessions are lost; fame disappears; relationships change; and health erodes over time. The good life that God has promised to us does not depend on circumstances. We can have joy in the midst of poverty, during failing health, and even during persecution.

God has laid out a prescription for the "good life" in Romans. This is done through a series of commands and spiritual principles describing how we should live after we have been saved. These principles for living are advice from God, provided for our good. They lead us to spiritually healthy living and relationships. Obeying God leads us away from what would harm us.

God's principles are not a guide for life in heaven but are a survival guide for Christians who live in a world still gripped by the power of sin. They show us how to avoid what is harmful, minimizing the consequences of sin. But these principles allow more than mere survival. They allow us to live a rich, abundant life, filled with joy and buoyed by hope regardless of our circumstances.

If we do not follow God's advice, if we do not take the medicine he has prescribed, there will be consequences. Those consequences will not affect our eternal destiny but will cause us to needlessly experience self-inflicted pain and suffering and to miss some of the blessings God has made available to us.

Section II has two chapters. The first chapter describes how we should live. This includes a new way of thinking, which incorporates God's values and perspectives. It also includes a new way of living that is pleasing to God and good for us.

The second chapter describes a new way of relating to people that is beneficial to us and to them. All of this is possible because we have a new spiritual nature and a new relationship with God.

Chapter 4

A New Way of Living

Servant

Paul, a servant of Christ Jesus. (Romans 1:1)

In this world,
we desire to give commands—not obey them.
We want to be served—not to serve.
We crave recognition—not obscurity.

In this world,
the notion of being a servant

- does not create aspirations

- does not generate envy

- does not inspire dreams

But in God's kingdom,
we are all servants of Jesus.
There is no greater position.
There is no more elevated status.
There is no higher calling.

In God's kingdom,
the role of a servant

- requires humility

- demands obedience

- embodies faithfulness

Let us who are servants of Jesus
quietly serve others with excellence
so that Jesus alone is glorified.
Let us who are servants of Jesus
Humbly serve others with dedication
so that Jesus alone is exalted.

Let us measure ourselves
by how many people we serve
in Jesus's name
and not by how many people serve us.

Let us identify ourselves
by our relationship to Jesus
and not by our position in this world.
Let us define ourselves
by what God has accomplished through us
and not what we have accomplished for ourselves.

Every Christian has the same status.
We all work in God's vineyard.
We are all servants of Jesus.
We all receive the same reward.

Live by Faith

For in the gospel the righteousness of God is revealed—a righteousness that is by faith from first to last, just as it is written: "The righteous will live by faith." (Romans 1:17)

We have been saved by faith,
so let us live by faith—
resting in the finished work of Christ,
knowing there is nothing we need to do
to earn or to keep our salvation

And as we live by faith,
we trust in the assurance of our salvation,
knowing it is a gift from God
that is forever with us

As we live by faith,
we never need to doubt
whether we are good enough,
for we were saved by God's grace—not by our merit.
We never need to wonder
if we have done enough,
for we were saved by God's grace—not by our works.
We never need to worry
if we will be able to finish the race,
for Jesus has already won the victory for us.

Live by faith,

knowing we were not saved because we were righteous

but saved so we could become righteous.

Live by faith,

knowing we did not earn salvation

but were given it by God's grace.

Unwavering Faith

Against all hope, Abraham in hope believed and so became the father of many nations … Without weakening in his faith, he faced the fact that his body was as good as dead—since he was about a hundred years old—and that Sarah's womb was also dead. Yet he did not waver through unbelief regarding the promise of God, but was strengthened in his faith and gave glory to God, being fully persuaded that God had power to do what he had promised. (Romans 4:18–21)

Faith is a gift from God—

the starter-dough of the bread of life

that will multiply and grow

as we exercise that faith—as we walk by faith.

When our faith is small,

we need a mountain of evidence

to take a little step of faith.

When our faith is small,

we need the assurance of past precedent

to trust in the future God has promised.

As we grow in faith,

we need less and less evidence

to take larger and larger steps of faith.

As we grow in faith,

we will trust in God's promises even when they

- are beyond our comprehension

- exceed our imagination

- surpass our dreams

Let us have faith like Abraham—
who believed all things are possible
with a sovereign God,
who believed all his promises are certain
with a faithful God.

When we have faith like Abraham,
waves of hopelessness can wash over us,
but faith will endure.
Torrents of disappointments can fall on us,
but faith will not waver.
Crushing grief can weigh us down,
but faith will remain.

When we have faith like Abraham,
Our faith in God's promises will not waver,
even when the voice of the past shouts
"It is impossible."
For the voice of faith says
"Nothing is impossible with God."

And as we walk with unwavering faith in God,
we see that faith always brings hope.
For as we trust in the assurance of his promises,
we look beyond momentary trouble and sorrow
and see heaven as clearly as the earth we walk upon.
We realize the future God has promised
is as certain as the past.

As we walk by faith, anchored by hope,
we realize that our frailty is not a liability
in fulfilling God's promises
but allows God's power to be fully displayed.

As we walk by faith, anchored by hope,
we realize that our weaknesses don't limit God
in accomplishing his purposes
but are opportunities for God to be glorified.

The Paradox of Grace

What shall we say, then? Shall we go on sinning so that grace may increase? By no means! We are those who have died to sin; how can we live in it any longer? (Romans 6:1–2)

The law made us crave freedom,
like a dog on a leash—
always pulling and tugging
to go where his nose leads.
But now,
having been freed from the law,
we willingly walk beside the One who loves us.

Sin made us crave what would harm us,
like an addict wanting the drugs that would kill him,
but now that we are free from sin's allure,
we are attracted to the things of God
That are good for us.

God's grace forever changed us.
We are like the avid shopper
who received a credit card with no limit
but now no longer desires what money can buy.

God's grace transformed us.
We are like the habitual criminal
who received a "get out of jail free card"
but now no longer wants to do what could imprison.

There is no going back
to where we used to live.
The old house has been demolished,
and a new one sits in its place.

There is no going back
to the old way of living.
Our life has a different trajectory.
Our life-journey has a new destination.

Here is the paradox of God's grace.
It frees us from the consequences of law-breaking
but changes us so we only wish to keep the law.
Here is the mystery of God's grace.
It does not lead to more and more sinning
but less and less.

Knowing Who We Are

> *For we know that our old self was crucified with him so that the body ruled by sin might be done away with, that we should no longer be slaves to sin—because anyone who has died has been set free from sin... In the same way, count yourselves dead to sin but alive to God in Christ Jesus. (Romans 6:6–7, 11)*

Some days

sin feels very much alive and powerful.

Some days

it feels like sin still reigns—looming over us.

Some days

we feel the cancer of our sin is merely in remission,

ready to return at any time.

And on those days,

we need to listen to what God has said

and not to whispers of our own doubt—

to self-serving judgments of others.

On those days,

we need to believe

we are who God has declared us to be

and not trust our unreliable feelings.

We may feel salvation changed nothing,

but God has said

we are new creatures in Christ.

We may think we are powerless to resist temptation,

but God has said

we are dead to sin and alive in Christ.

We may think there is no meaning in our lives,
but God has said
he has called us for his purposes.

Let us live a new life,
knowing we have been transformed.
Because we are alive in Christ
we are dead to sin.
Because we have died with Christ
sin has no power over us,
except that which we choose to give it.

As we trust God's proclamation
that sin has been defeated—
as we live out the truth
that we are dead to sin—
the spiritual transformation within
will be displayed in our lives.
Hope will replace anxiety—peace will reign.
Love will prevail over apathy.

Grace Living

Do not let sin reign in your mortal body so that you obey its evil desires. Do not offer any part of yourself to sin as an instrument of wickedness, but rather offer yourselves to God …and offer every part of yourself to him as an instrument of righteousness. For sin shall no longer be your master, because you are not under the law, but under grace. (Romans 6:12–14)

God has declared

we are no longer under the tyranny of sin

but are citizens of the kingdom of righteousness.

God has declared

his grace is not a license to continue in sin

but freedom to sin no more.

God has declared

we are dead to sin

and alive to him.

Choose to enjoy the freedom

we have been given by God's grace!

Why would we allow sin to dominate us

after Christ has set us free from its power?

Why would we continue to work for the slave master

after we have been set free?

Rejoice that we have been forgiven!

Why would we carry a burden of guilt

after Christ has paid the penalty for our sin?

Why would we be like a debtor

who continues to make loan payments

after the debt has been paid?

We must hold up our heads as children of God!
Why would we allow sin to shame us
since God no longer condemns us?
Why would we continue to live in the shadows
after being acquitted?

May we love to grow in righteousness
even though we will never fully achieve it.
May we love to obey the law
even though we won't meet its standard.
May we want to do right
even in those times when we fail.

The Struggle

I have the desire to do what is good, but I cannot carry it out. For I do not do the good I want to do, but the evil I do not want to do—this I keep on doing. Now if I do what I do not want to do, it is no longer I who do it, but it is sin living in me that does it... Although I want to do good, evil is right there with me. (Romans 7:18–21)

Christ has won the war.

He has secured the victory.

Sin has been defeated for us.

The power of sin in us has been broken.

And yet we who have been saved

struggle with sin.

Do not let the struggle with sin

cause us to doubt our salvation.

If the power of sin had not been broken,

there would be no struggle.

Sin would be our friend and companion.

We would run to sin and embrace its temptations.

Let us see that the struggle with sin

is evidence of our salvation,

for only the saved want to resist.

Let us remember that

we are free from the power of sin

but not its presence.

Until our last day on earth, we will be tempted.

Until our final breath,

we will battle sin.

Let us not think the saved are sinless,
for that only feeds our pride
and starves the humility that we need.
Let us not think the saved are sinless,
for that causes us to deny our sin,
never seeking the cleansing of forgiveness.

Let us not think sinning is inevitable,
for that leads to living a defeated life,
never expecting victory over sin.
Then sin does defeat us, and we sin more and more.

Let us live on this earth,
knowing that temptation cannot be avoided
but God has provided an escape from sin.
Knowing that we want to do good
but may not always succeed.

We thank Jesus Christ our Savior,
that our eternal destiny is not determined
by our ability to be good,
but by the righteousness of Christ imputed to us.

Sharing in Christ's Sufferings

Now if we are children, then we are heirs—heirs of God and co-heirs with Christ, if indeed we share in his sufferings in order that we may also share in his glory. I consider that our present sufferings are not worth comparing with the glory that will be revealed in us. (Romans 8:17–18)

Jesus did not seek suffering, did not relish pain,
but was willing to endure it—
not for himself but for his Father,
not for himself but for our sakes.

Jesus did not suffer for personal gain
but suffered so we could gain salvation.
Jesus did not suffer in the pursuit of glory
but endured affliction for the glory of God the Father.

Jesus did not suffer for doing wrong
but was afflicted for doing what is right.
Jesus did not suffer because it was unavoidable
but willingly endured pain and anguish for us.

We don't need to seek that kind of suffering.
It finds us when we do the work of Christ.
Just like Christ

- we will be ridiculed

- we will be rejected

- we will be despised

And when we suffer like Christ—
it is because we are doing what is right.
And when we suffer for Christ—
it is because the world sees him in us.

There is no good in suffering itself.
God himself has promised
there will be a time when there is no more pain.
Christ himself has prepared a place
where there will be no more suffering.

Sharing in Christ's suffering
is the road we must travel
for good to be done—for God's purposes to be achieved.
This kind of suffering is well worth the pain.
Like the pain of child birth is willingly endured
to bring new life into the world.
Like the exhaustion of training is freely withstood
to win the race.

Let us not fear suffering for Christ.
Let us not flee from it
but face it without hesitation.
We know that momentary sharing in Christ's sufferings
is the road all the saved will travel.
We know that when we share in his sufferings,
we will share in his glory.

Sharing the Gospel

> *How, then, can they call on the one they have not believed in? And how can they believe in the one of whom they have not heard? And how can they hear without someone preaching to them? And how can anyone preach unless they are sent? As it is written: "How beautiful are the feet of those who bring good news!" (Romans 10:14–15)*

Everyone who has placed their faith in Jesus

- has been given a calling

- has a purpose and place in Christ's church

- has a role to play in God's plan.

But regardless of our specific calling,

regardless of our unique purpose,

every Christian is a messenger of the gospel.

We have been empowered to share the good news—

entrusted with a message of hope.

Every Christian has a unique testimony to share,

a personal story to tell—

how they were saved,

what Jesus has done in their lives.

There is no greater privilege
than being a messenger of the gospel,
for we carry the word of God.
The gospel is

- a beacon of hope to the hopeless

- a message of deliverance to the perishing

- a word of life to the dying

God has good news for the world—
a glorious message of salvation,
and he has chosen us—the rescued—
to deliver that message to the perishing.

Let us share the gospel with passion,
having experienced the transformation in our lives.
Let us share the gospel with compassion,
having witnessed the destruction of sin.
Let us share the gospel with urgency,
knowing the certainty of God's wrath.

Let us share the gospel with the same urgency
as if we were carrying the only antidote
for a person dying of poison.
Let us share the gospel with the same conviction
as a former drug addict telling kids
how to avoid the destruction he experienced.

Let us see the vital nature of our calling—

the urgency of our witness.

Now is the time for boldness.

Now is the time for diligence.

We know not when the end will come.

With it, the opportunity for salvation will be lost.

Do not let our weaknesses

cause us to falter as messengers of the gospel.

Use them as an opportunity

to fully trust in the power of the gospel message.

Do not let our failures

be the reason we are timid in sharing God's good news.

Let our past failures be the basis of our testimony

as to what God has done in our lives.

Avoiding Arrogance

> *Do not be arrogant, but tremble. For if God did not spare the natural branches, he will not spare you either. Consider therefore the kindness and sternness of God: sternness to those who fell, but kindness to you, provided that you continue in his kindness. Otherwise, you also will be cut off. (Romans 11:20–22)*

How can we prevent
spiritual pride from slithering into our hearts—
whispering we are worthier than others?
How can we resist
the allure of self-righteous arrogance—
tempting us to think that we are better than
those whose sins are more apparent?

We can stay humble
by considering both God's kindness and his sternness.
We will be grateful
as we remember all God's kindnesses
given by his mercy.
We will be grateful
as we reflect on his terrible judgment
God has spared us from by his grace.

Pride cannot coexist with gratitude.
How is there room for pride
when we realize we are spared from judgment
only by God's grace?
How can we be arrogant
when we know our very existence
depends on God's mercy?

May we never presume upon God's kindness
but fear his sternness.
Remember—
he is a God of both judgment and mercy.
Remember—
God created both heaven and hell.

Consider the fullness of God's character,
for he is both relentless in wrath
and overflowing with compassion.
Let us live in obedience to God,
both by gratitude for his mercy
and fear of his wrath

As we remember the power of God's terrible wrath—
His sternness in judgment—
we bow before God with reverent fear.
But that fear increases our love for him
as we realize that it is only his grace
that stands between us and his judgment.
May our consideration of the reality of hell
make God's gift of salvation even sweeter.

A Living Sacrifice

> *Therefore, I urge you, brothers and sisters, in view of God's*
> *mercy, to offer your bodies as a living sacrifice, holy and pleasing*
> *to God—this is your true and proper worship. (Romans 12:1)*

How do we respond to the wonder of God's mercy?
For God

- pardoned us even though we were guilty

- loved us when we were his enemies

- found us when we were lost

- rescued us when we were perishing

- gave life to our spirits when they were dead.

How do we respond to God
in light of all that he has done for us?

- is gratitude enough?

- is praise sufficient?

- is obedience necessary?

Let our response include a heart full of gratitude.
We can never thank God enough
for all he was done.
Let our voice be filled with words of praise,
for God is worthy of all praise—
eternity is not long enough to recite all his wonders.

But let our worship be more than emotion—
more than just words.
Let us live the life God has given us
in a way that pleases him.
Let us be a living sacrifice—
not reluctantly yielding our bodies
but willingly presenting our lives to God.
For the offer is not
a sacrifice of appeasement to be saved
but a sacrifice of gratitude because we have been saved.

And as we live sacrificially for God,
we taste the delicious paradox of God's grace.
As we humble ourselves before God,
he will exalt us.
As we submit our will to God's,
he will give us what fulfills us.
As we offer to God a life destined for death,
he will give us eternal life.

The Choice

> *Do not conform to the pattern of this world, but be transformed*
> *by the renewing of your mind. (Romans 12:2)*

We who have been saved by God's grace
have a choice as to how we live—
whether to be conformed or to be transformed.
Whether to be conformed to the ways of the world
or transformed to the ways of Christ.

The world is continually working to mold us

- tempting us where we are weakest
- threatening us where we are most vulnerable

But we are no longer the world's playdough.
Now that we have been saved,
we have a choice.
Our lives can be transformed—we can have better lives.

It all starts with the mind.
What we believe
determines how we live.
No one reaches the top of the mountain
unless they believe they can.
No one changes their life
unless they believe it is possible.

Spiritual renewal begins with knowing the truth.

Truth comes from God' word.

Truth about the nature of humanity—the nature of God.

How all things began—how they will end.

Truth about what we should do

and what we should avoid.

Let us apply to our lives

the truth we have come to know and to believe,

for belief always results in action—

faith in God always produces obedience to God.

The world will present us with temptation,

wanting us to stumble—to give in.

But now we will be able to resist,

knowing God has said

he will provide a way of escape.

The world will threaten us with punishment,

wanting to bully us into silence—

intimidate us into acquiescence.

But now we will be able to continue in courage,

for we know God has told us

do not be afraid—he is with us always.

The world will ratchet up the pressure,

desiring to paralyze us with anxiety and worry.

But now we are able to act with confident assurance,

believing God's promise that

he will provide—he will protect.

The world will taunt us with past failures,

wanting us to doubt we can ever change.

But now we will not listen—we will not be discouraged.

We will give up the old lifestyle,

believing God's promise

that we are new creatures in Christ.

Let us be transformed

so we can be in the world but not of the world.

Let us be transformed by Christ

so we can transform the world for Christ.

As we continually renew our minds,

the world will not be changing us,

but instead we will be changing the world.

Know the Will of God

Be transformed by the renewing of your mind. Then you will be able to test and approve what God's will is—his good, pleasing and perfect will. (Romans 12:2)

We wonder—
what is God's will for us?
What is his plan for us?
We ponder

- who to marry

- what job to take

- what house to buy.

Let us realize that how we conduct ourselves in marriage
is more important than who we marry.
Let us see that being content with our house, our job,
is more important than which house—which job.
God's will does not focus on circumstances
but how we respond to them.

We cannot know the future—
except that which the prophets have revealed.
Focus on living righteously in the present
rather than idle speculation about the future.
Strive to live righteously wherever God has placed us
rather than worrying about where we should live.

What is God's will for us?

- that we follow the guidance of the Holy Spirit

- that we obey God's commands

- that we love him and love one another

Accept God's invitation to test his will.
Live like Christ. Obey God's commands.
Submit to God's will.
See what God will do.

Then we will come to realize
that God's will is perfect.
Then we will see there is no better way to live
than God's way.
Then we will experience
joy in obeying God's commands,
and we will be able to look at our life and be satisfied—
never regretting our obedience

Not Too High—Not Too Low

Do not think of yourself more highly than you ought, but rather think of yourself with sober judgment, in accordance with the faith God has distributed to each of you. (Romans 12:3)

Let us not think too highly of ourselves,
magnifying our strength, minimizing our weakness.
Then we puff up with pride—
elevating ourselves in our own minds,
thinking others should serve us,
thinking others should praise us.

Let us not think too lowly of ourselves,
believing our lives are worthless, our abilities useless.
Then we sink into despair and self-loathing,
becoming incapable of helping others
and convincing ourselves we have nothing to offer.

Let us not think of ourselves too highly or too lowly,
for neither makes us useful in God's kingdom.
Both views are self-centered.
Both want to be served rather than serving others.

To guard against an assessment that is too low,
remember that God

- created us in his image

- loves us unconditionally

- gave us eternal life

To guard against an assessment that is too high,
remember that

- all of us have sinned

- none of us are worthy of salvation

- all of us have been saved only by God's grace

- all of us are equal in God's sight

May God give us the courage to be honest
for only the truth can free us from:

- the deceit of our own hearts

- being puffed up by well-intentioned flattery

- being torn down by the lies told about us.

May God give us discernment
to see our weaknesses
and to praise God that he loves us despite them.
May God give us discernment
to see our strengths
and to thank God for his gift.
May God give us courage
to accept the truth of who we are
and to trust that God is able to transform us.

Zealous Service

Never be lacking in zeal, but keep your spiritual fervor, serving the Lord. (Romans 12:11)

When our passion to serve in the name of Jesus
is fueled
by the anticipation of rewards—
by a hunger for recognition,
that zeal will disappear when

- the applause dies

- our work goes unnoticed

- the only recognition is criticism

- we see no accomplishments for our efforts

But when our passion for helping others
is fueled by gratitude to God,
we will not become apathetic or discouraged when

- adversity engulfs us

- friends abandon support

- enemies persist in their attacks

Our gratitude is continually replenished
by God's unending acts of kindness.
Our love for others does not cease
when it is God's love flowing through us.

Our zeal in serving God
comes from gratitude for his goodness
and not to earn his favor.
Our obedience to God
derives from our love for him
and not to merit his love.

Joyful Hope

Be joyful in hope. (Romans 12:12)

When our joy is found
in the shallow soil of circumstances,
it will be

- uprooted by the winds of adversity

- withered in the hot sun of suffering

- stunted by the darkness of difficulties

But our joy comes from hope
in the return of Jesus Christ.
It is no mere wish—no fanciful dream
but a future more certain than yesterday's sunrise.
God himself has proclaimed Christ's return,
and God's word never fails; it is eternally true.

This hope is the rock that cannot be moved—
the light that cannot be extinguished,
and this great hope fills us with joy
for what is to come—for what has been promised.

It is a persistent joy that is not extinguished
by the winds of adversity.
It is a self-renewing joy that is not consumed
by the demands and stresses in our lives.
It is a buoyant joy that is not pulled under
by the riptides of despair.

Only the perspective of that hope
allows us to see our troubles
as light and momentary.
Only from the high vantage point of hope
will we see our adversity as small and insignificant.

Patient in Pain

Be ... patient in affliction. (Romans 12:12)

We try to avoid pain and suffering.
But when they are inescapable,
we want them to end as quickly as possible.
Then we cry out to God,
for the pain to stop—for the suffering to cease.
We pray that

- our cancer will be healed

- the scars of divorce will disappear

- the bullying will end

And we should cry out to God
in our times of pain and affliction.
But let us be patient as we wait for God's response.
God acts in times and ways of his choosing—
has purposes hidden from our understanding.

Such patience is not natural but supernatural.
But when we patiently endure that pain,
we will hear the whisper of God
speaking words of comfort and encouragement.
When we patiently endure that suffering,
we will see God working for our good
in the worst situations—in the direst circumstances.

As we are patient in affliction,
this endurance is a testimony of faith
more powerful than words—
demonstrating who we are and what we believe
to a world that is watching and listening.

In our patient endurance,
we proclaim our trust in God
that he will be with us in every adversity.
We announce our confidence
that God will cause good to result.
We show our faith
that God's promises will be fulfilled.
It is a testimony that we believe what we say.

Wisdom and Innocence

I want you to be wise about what is good, and innocent about what is evil. (Romans 16:19)

Let us steep our minds in God's truth
until its flavors and aroma
permeate every crevice.
Let us fill our minds with pure and holy thoughts
until there is no room for anything else.

Let us strive to know the depth of God's goodness
and not explore the limits of evil.
Let us ponder on ways to do what is right
and not investigate the boundary of sin.
Let us study God's word
and not the ways of the world.

Let us realize there is no value
in studying the intricacies of sin—the dimensions of evil,
but let it be sufficient
that we recognize what is evil
simply because it is not of God.

Let us hunger to know God's word
and long to always be in his presence.
As we study God's word—
spend time with him in prayer
our hearts and minds will be transformed.
We will understand God's ways—
His truth will be revealed.

Chapter 5

New Relationships with Others

Unity in Diversity

For just as each of us has one body with many members, and these members do not all have the same function, so in Christ we, though many, form one body, and each member belongs to all the others. (Romans 12:4–5)

There is only one body of Christ—one church—
and it is God who

- calls each of us into that body

- makes us members

- assigns our part of the whole

In Christ's church,
we don't all look alike,
but we are united by one Lord.
We don't all think alike,
but we are united by one Spirit.
We don't all share the same language,
but we are united by one faith.

Whether we are a man or a woman,
child or centenarian, rich or poor,
illiterate or educated, conservative or liberal,
we are all one in the body of Christ.

Let us realize what unites us
is far greater than what would divide us.
Let us remember we all

- share the same faith

- serve the same Lord

- have the same hope

Then our unity as Christians
will begin now on the earth
and continue into heaven's eternity.

Beauty from Brokenness

> *So in Christ we, though many, form one body, and each member belongs to all the others. (Romans 12:5)*

We were like pieces of pottery,
broken from the fall,
worthless shards,
each with a unique shape—a different size.

But from humanity's pile of rubble,
the Master Artisan carefully picks each piece,
placing it where our jagged edges
fit perfectly next to our brothers'.
And from our shattered lives
God creates a beautiful mosaic—
his church.

From the worthless rubble of broken lives,
God created a priceless mosaic.
From the chaos of disparate lives,
God produced a pleasing harmony.
From our brokenness,
God created beauty.

Purpose and Place

For just as each of us has one body with many members, and these members do not all have the same function, so in Christ we, though many, form one body. (Romans 12:4-5)

Each of us
has a place in Christ's church.
God himself has chosen us and placed us there.
Each of us is a note
in a symphony written by the Master Composer.
Each of us is a thread
in the tapestry designed by the Master Weaver.
Each of us is a word
in the book written by the Great Author.
Together,
we become the church

- designed by God

- constructed by God

- sustained by God

A single word does not tell a story,
but the book is incomplete with missing words.
One note does not make a melody,
but the music lacks harmony absent all the notes.
So too each member in the body of Christ
has significance and purpose.

We trust the Master Composer
has put our note in just the right place
to fulfill the intended harmony.
We trust the Master Weaver
has placed the thread of our life
in just the right place
to complete the tapestry's story.

Belonging to One Another

So in Christ we, though many, form one body, and each member belongs to all the others. (Romans 12:5)

Let us live the truth
that we are Team Jesus.
We have the same aspirations.
We have been chosen and assembled
for the same purpose—seek the same victory.
We lift our teammates when they fall.
We rejoice with them when they succeed.

Let us live the truth
that we belong to one another.
Acknowledging
we have a time to give and a time to receive—
a time to help and a time to be helped.

Let us live the truth
that we are brothers and sisters in God's family.
Do not allow conflict to separate us—
but have relationships that will endure,
for your sibling is always your sibling.

Live the truth that we united by Christ—
living in community.
Realize that we are stronger together
than facing struggles and trials separately.

As we live life together, bound by Christ's love,
we realize that we were not meant to live alone,
for it is God who has joined us together.

As we see we belong to one another in Christ,
we will desire to seek relationships
more than we fear rejection.

As we realize we belong to one another,
we will support one another in our struggles
and cling to one another in times of adversity.

God's Orchestra

We have different gifts, according to the grace given to each of us. If your gift is prophesying, then prophesy in accordance with your faith; if it is serving, then serve; if it is teaching, then teach; if it is to encourage, then give encouragement; if it is giving, then give generously; if it is to lead, do it diligently; if it is to show mercy, do it cheerfully. (Romans 12:6–8)

The gospel
is like a glorious symphony composed by God—
music that lifts us from earth into heaven itself.
The church
is like an orchestra playing that symphony
with God as its conductor
and every Christian as a musician.

Whether you play the high or low notes,
whether you add to the rhythm or play the melody,
every musician adds to the richness of the sound—
has an essential part of the performance.

Some are more talented—some are more experienced,
but each of us has our assigned place
in God's orchestra.
Each of us has a part to play
in God's symphony.

Let us recognize our place
and play our part with joy and gusto.
Let us rejoice in our role
and play our best for the glory of God.

Gifted for One Another

We have different gifts, according to the grace given to each of us. If your gift is prophesying, then prophesy in accordance with your faith; if it is serving, then serve; if it is teaching, then teach; if it is to encourage, then give encouragement; if it is giving, then give generously; if it is to lead, do it diligently; if it is to show mercy, do it cheerfully. (Romans 12:6-8)

In his grace,
God has given each of us a spiritual gift—a special talent
to build up the body of Christ.
The primary purpose of each gift
is not to enrich ourselves but for the benefit of others.

Spiritual gifts only exist in community—
can only be exercised within relationships.
How can teachers teach without students?
How can leaders lead unless there are followers?
How can givers give unless someone has a need?

As we realize our gifts
are for the good of others and for the glory of God,
we will look for opportunities
to use the gift God has given us—
to fulfill a unique purpose in his plans.

Value and respect the spiritual gifts of others,
knowing each gift is essential
for the whole work of the church to be done.
Know that God gave those gifts to others
with the same thought and care as our own.

Use our gifts to serve others,
for that is what God intended.
Let us use our gifts to their full potential,
for they were given to us by God for a purpose.
Let us use our gifts diligently,
for our time on earth is short.
Let us use our gifts faithfully,
for God is worthy.

Authentic Love

Love must be sincere. (Romans 12:9)

We used to mimic love
like actors in play—
wearing a mask of politeness, a veneer of conformity
to cover a selfish heart.
Counterfeit love cost us little
and changed us less.
But deceit's reward is not treasure in heaven.
The wages of fictitious love
are only the fleeting praise of the deceived.

But as we experienced God's unconditional love—
who loved as we were
then we were changed,
and we were able to truly love others.

Let our love be authentic—let it be real

- putting the needs of others before our own

- doing what is best for them—not best for us

- doing more than expected—more than they ask

Let our love be genuine

- willing to be anonymous

- seeking no glory

- wanting no recognition for itself

Let us love like Jesus Christ our Lord
who sought only to bring glory to the Father.

Let our love be authentic,
motivated by compassion—not driven by duty,
like Jesus Christ our redeemer
who willingly went to the cross
because he loved us.

Let our love be sincere,
expecting nothing in return.
Let our love be sacrificial,
willing to pay a cost for another.
Let our love be like Jesus's love.

Faithful in Prayer

Be ... faithful in prayer. (Romans 12:12)

Never stop praying,
for prayer is an ongoing expression of faith
that God

- hears our prayers

- cares about our circumstances

- will answer them in accordance with his will

Never stop praying,
for prayer is a continual expression of humility
that we depend on God
at all times and in all circumstances.

Never stop praying,
for prayer is an ongoing expression of gratitude
for all that God has done—and all that he will do.
Prayer is unending praise
for who God is.

And as we are faithful in prayer,
God will be faithful to respond.
He is our Father

- who always hears our voices

- who loves to give good things to his children

Always Hospitable

> *Share with the Lord's people who are in need. Practice hospitality. (Romans 12:13)*

Hospitality is opening our hearts,
our doors, our hands to those in need.
And who does not have needs?
Who does not need

- to receive a warm smile?

- to hear a kind word?

- to receive an act of kindness?

And as we share—as we show hospitality
By welcoming people into our lives—
then the melancholy of hoarding
is replaced with cheerful giving.
The sorrow of solitude
gives way to the joy of connection.

Inhospitality is a trap.
It only reminds of us what we don't have,
while the hospitable heart
treasures all that God has given us.

Practice hospitality with repetition,
pursue it with diligence, and perform it with joy.
Let hospitality be an intentional way of life
and not as an accidental occurrence.
Look for reasons to show hospitality,
seizing every opportunity—
not making up excuses why we cannot.

Hospitality done in love
wants nothing in return—
expects no reciprocity.
Hospitality done with love
causes others to feel accepted.

Hospitality has no agenda
except to make people feel loved.
Hospitality has no schedule
except those encounters ordained by God.
Hospitality has no grand purpose
except to love people one at a time.

Hospitality requires no special skill—
no unique personality, no designated location.
God provides the opportunities.
God gives us the desire. God empowers us to act.

Everyone can be hospitable.
It need be no more than

- giving a friendly smile

- sharing an encouraging word

- including another in our conversation

Be Empathetic

Rejoice with those who rejoice; mourn with those who mourn.
(Romans 12:15)

A bond is forged in the warmth of shared laughter.
A connection is made in the mingling of tears.
Whether we soar together in the heights of joy
or trudge through the depths of sorrow,
our hearts are joined in that moment.

When we share in the emotions of others,
we don't look down with disdain
at someone overwhelmed with sorrow,
and we don't look up with envy
at someone overjoyed with his or her blessings.
But we look across at one another
whose heart beats with our hearts.

When we drink from the same emotional cup,
it demonstrates mutual trust and understanding.
Empathy is

- more than spending time together

- more than providing money

- more than giving advice

It is walking down the road of life together,
enjoying the same sunshine, enduring the same storms.

Empathy has no verticality,
for it only exists in the horizontal.
Empathy knows no separation,
for its bond transcends time and space.

Let us be like Jesus.
He spent time with people
in their nights of despair and in the days of joy.
Jesus

- had compassion on the sick and the hurting

- gave hope to those who had none

- showed the way to those who were lost

Whether they were strangers or friends,
whether they were Jews or Gentiles,
whether they agreed or disagreed,
Jesus joined in with their laughter
and shared in their tears.

As disciples of Jesus,
we can have empathy like his
as we follow his template—
walk in the trail he has blazed.

Bless Our Persecutors

Bless those who persecute you; bless and do not curse… "If your enemy is hungry, feed him; if he is thirsty, give him something to drink." (Romans 12:14, 20)

We are called to bless those who persecute us—
asking God to do something good
for those who oppress and harass us.
We are called to pray for God's blessings on those

- who lie about us

- who ridicule us

- who cheat us

More than praying for God's blessings,
God calls us
to help our enemies in their times of need—
help those who would harm us if they could.

This kind of love
is not natural but supernatural.
This kind of love
does not naturally spring from our hearts
but only comes from God.

We are able to love our enemies
only because God first loved us—
while we were still his enemies.
And as we love our persecutors,
we no longer fear them—
for who can fear the ones they love?

We are able to forgive our enemies
only because God has already forgiven us,
and once we forgive our persecutors,
we are freed from the prison of bitterness.

We are able to bless our persecutors
because God has abundantly blessed us.
And as we bless them, we see them as God sees them,
not the towering stature of the powerful
but as hurting and needy people.

May we be able to bless our persecutors
the way Christ blessed those who persecuted him.
While he was dying on the cross,
Jesus asked his Father to forgive those who

- hated him without cause

- plotted to kill him

- arrested him without charge

- placed him on the cross to die

May we be able to bless
those kinds of people in our lives

Be Humble

Do not be proud, but be willing to associate with people of low position. Do not be conceited. (Romans 12:16)

We are attracted to the powerful, drawn to the wealthy,
and enamored with the famous.
We are eager to associate
with those who can lift us up.

But what about those people
with a lower status—with less money, less popularity?
But what about those people
who have nothing to offer us
except demands for our time,
our money, our emotional support?

Are we so proud
that we don't have time for those in need?
Are we so conceited
that we refuse to associate with those less fortunate?
Are we so self-righteous
that we avoid those with sins more visible than our own?
May it never be!

Jesus
always had time for those in need,
even when he had no time to give.
Jesus
continuously cared for society's outcasts
even when no one else would.
Jesus
willingly associated with sinners
against the indignant protest of the religious.

Jesus did not isolate himself from the world,
nor did he engage in the sinful acts of the world.
Jesus humbled himself to our level,
loving the unlovable, accepting the rejected.
Jesus drew the world to himself one person at a time
by healing the hurting, helping the needy,
people like you, and people like me.

As we humble ourselves like Jesus,
we will see the invisible people all around us
who we had never noticed before.
We will remember the forgotten
pushed from memory
by our chosen busyness.

As we live like Jesus,
we will stop talking about ourselves
and start listening to the needs of others.
We will acknowledge our weaknesses
so we can have compassion for others.

Live at Peace with Others

> *If it is possible, as far as it depends on you, live at peace with everyone. (Romans 12:18)*
>
> *Let us therefore make every effort to do what leads to peace and to mutual edification. (Romans 14:19)*

We are often at war with others.

A war

- sparked by hurts

- fueled by misunderstanding

- flamed by retaliation

And when there is war,
there is no peace—only conflict.
There is no harmony—only hostility.
There is no rest—only fighting.

Peace with God is a gift—given by his grace.
But if we want peace with others, we must work for it.
We must be the ones
who remove obstacles—clear up misunderstandings.
We must be the ones
who humble ourselves by admitting our faults.
We must be the ones
who are willing to forgive
without expecting we will be forgiven.

We can plant the seeds of peace—
create an environment where peace can grow—
but we cannot cause the plant to bear fruit.
Regardless of what we do,
there is no assurance there will be peace,
for the other person must want it.

We can build a bridge of peace,
but the other must cross over it.
We can tear a hole in barriers that divide,
but the other must walk through it.

For God
did everything necessary to reconcile us,
but we must believe in Jesus as our Savior.
For God
offers us peace through Jesus's sacrifice,
but we must accept it.
We who have been given peace with God
must offer peace to others.
We who have been reconciled to God
must work to reconcile with our enemies.

Let God Avenge

Do not take revenge, my dear friends, but leave room for God's wrath, for it is written: "It is mine to avenge; I will repay," says the Lord. (Romans 12:19)

We do not need to be taught revenge.
It is in our nature

- to take vengeance against those who wrong us

- to hurt those who hurt us

- to repay evil with evil

When we have been wronged,
sin twists our God-given desire for justice
into a hunger for revenge.
But when we seek to satisfy that hunger,
the sweetness of our revenge quickly turns bitter.
Revenge's salve does not heal our wounds
but becomes poison that kills our souls.

Our revenge does not

- sooth the sting of injustice

- restore what has been destroyed

- bring peace

Revenge only perpetuates a cycle of violence.
That is why God has said,
"Do not take revenge."
That is why God has said
he will avenge—he will repay.
That is why God has promised
there will be justice.

It is the certainty of God's wrath
that allows us to escape the bitterness that comes

- when our enemies do not make amends

- when there is no repentance from wrongdoers

- when there is no evidence of justice

It is the certainty of God's wrath
that allows us

- to lay down the burden of anger

- to forgive those who have hurt us

- to love even our enemies

One day
there will be vengeance,
but not by our hands.
God will be our avenger,
and every wrong will be righted

One day
there will be justice,
but this is not the time.
God's judgment is coming,
and his justice will prevail.

Love without Ceasing

Let no debt remain outstanding, except the continuing debt to love one another, for whoever loves others has fulfilled the law. (Romans 13:8)

We cannot love someone too much.

We cannot love someone too long.

No one is beyond the limits of our love.

No one is excluded from our love.

We have an ongoing obligation to love others.

We have a debt that can never be repaid.

Let us love others
the way God loves us.
God's love

- never ceases

- has no boundary

- needs no prompting

- requires no response

Let us love others

- even when we do not feel like loving

- even when all our love has been consumed

- even when our own needs are not satisfied

May our love increase even more,
as the needs of others around us grow.

God's love
falls upon us like rain,
continually replenishing our reservoir of love
until it overflows
into acts of kindness and compassion.

Loving Your Neighbors

> *The commandments ... are summed up in this one command: "Love your neighbor as yourself." Love does no harm to a neighbor. Therefore love is the fulfillment of the law. (Romans 13:9–10)*

Let us not give love
like a banker making a loan—
expecting to be repaid with interest—
for then there is no joy in receiving love,
only repayment of what is owed.
But let us love others expecting nothing in return,
for that is how God loves us.

Let us not give love
in proportion to the love received,
for that is not how God loves us.
Let our love be unconditional—
be selfless and not self-serving.

God has called us
to love our neighbors as ourselves,
meaning we treat everyone
the way we want to be treated—
with kindness, with compassion, with respect.
It means we love everyone we meet
in the way we want to be loved—
an unconditional love irrespective of merit,
independent of reciprocation.

To love our neighbors as ourselves
means we continue to serve others
even when they do not appreciate our sacrifice—
even when they are unworthy of it,
for this is how God loved us.

To love our neighbors as ourselves
means we forgive others again and again,
even when they continue to offend us,
even when we still feel the pain of their wrongdoing,
for this is how God has forgiven us.

Be Awake

> *Let no debt remain outstanding, except the continuing debt to love one another, for whoever loves others has fulfilled the law … And do this, understanding the present time: The hour has already come for you to wake up from your slumber, because our salvation is nearer now than when we first believed. The night is nearly over; the day is almost here. So let us put aside the deeds of darkness and put on the armor of light. (Romans 13:8, 11–12)*

We live in this twilight
when the age of sin is ending
and the age of righteousness is dawning.
We live in this twilight
when the promised return of Christ is imminent
but not yet here.

How should we live in this present time?

- when sin still exists but is no longer our master

- when Satan still lives but has been defeated

- when death still strikes but we have eternal life

How do we live in the time of almost but not yet?

It is the time of spiritual warfare.
Even though Christ has already won the victory

- over sin

- over the devil

- over death

the victory will not be consummated—war will not end
until Christ returns.

With his return,
the age of God's mercy concludes
and his judgment commences.
Let us not sleep while the battle still rages—
but awake from our slumber.
There is still time to make a difference.
Eternal destinies still hang in the balance
for the souls of our family, our neighbors, our friends.

Let us who have seen Christ's light
not cling to the darkness, linger in sin's shadow,
toying with temptation.
Let us walk boldly in the light,
rejecting the world's dark rewards.

Do not waste the time God has given us
on self-indulgence and self-gratification.
Do not squander the opportunities
God has provided to proclaim his gospel.
There is no greater act of love
than to share the gospel to the perishing.
Now is the time for salvation,
for this is the age of the Lord's grace.

Don't Let Doctrine Divide

Accept the one whose faith is weak, without quarreling over disputable matters. One person's faith allows them to eat anything, but another, whose faith is weak, eats only vegetables. The one who eats everything must not treat with contempt the one who does not, and the one who does not eat everything must not judge the one who does, for God has accepted them. (Romans 14:1–3)

There is only one church called by God,

but within that one church

there are deep differences

regarding how we should live.

Christians with a broad view of their freedom in Christ,

believe that everything is permissible

except that specifically prohibited by God.

Believe they have the freedom

to eat or drink whatever they want,

to do whatever they want, to say whatever they choose.

Christians with a narrow view of their liberty,

believe they should do

only what is expressly permitted by God.

Believe they would be sinning

by participating in certain activities—

by saying certain things.

We pray
that liberal Christians will not ridicule
those with the narrow view for their abstinence
but will accept them as fellow believers.
We pray
that conservative Christians will not judge
those with the broader view for their actions
but will also accept them as brothers and friends.

For how can either
reject those whom God has chosen?
If a holy and righteous God has saved someone—
who are we to reject them?
If God has adopted them into his family,
who are we to disown them?

But God has commanded all of us
to accept fellow Christians
with opinions and preferences different from our own—
not merely tolerate
but welcome them as friends and as brothers.
Let us realize these current differences
will disappear in eternity,
for there will be no
liberal or conservative Christians in heaven,
just followers of Jesus.

Let us not be legalistic in our liberalism
and insist everybody should do what we do—
should embrace what we embrace.
Let us not be judgmental in our conservatism
and insist no one should do what we condemn—
should practice the same abstinence as we do.

May God guard both liberal and conservative Christians
from divisive pride—
each believing they are right,
each believing their way is best.
Who among us
perfectly understands God's word?
Who among us
always does what is right?

Judge or Judged?

> *You, then, why do you judge your brother or sister? Or why do you treat them with contempt? For we will all stand before God's judgment seat... So then, each of us will give an account of ourselves to God. (Romans 14:10, 12)*

God has said
we are all brothers and sisters in Christ.
But too often
we want to assume the role of older brother—
presume to act as the older sister
in the family of God.

God has said
we are all equal in Christ.
But too often
we want to be first among equals
in the work God has called us to do.
Too often
we want to play the role of judge—
to be the one to determine right and wrong,
to be the one to pronounce judgment,
and yet it is we who will be judged by God.

Let us not judge with contempt
fellow Christians who exercise their liberty
to do what we believe is wrong in the sight of God.
Let us not judge with ridicule
fellow believers who abstain
from that we think God would find acceptable.

Do not forget—
it is we who will be judged by God.
Do not forget—
it is we who will be held accountable by God.
Do not forget—
God alone is worthy to be judge of all.

Let us focus on our own actions
and not be critics of others.
Let us focus on our obedience to God
and not monitor the conduct of others.

Love over Liberty

> *Make up your mind not to put any stumbling block or obstacle in the way of a brother or sister... If your brother or sister is distressed because of what you eat, you are no longer acting in love. Do not by your eating destroy someone for whom Christ died. (Romans 14:13, 15)*

Let those who are strong in faith
never flaunt their liberty
if it tempts their conservative brother
to do what he believes is wrong—
if it causes stress and division
in the body of Christ.

Let those who are strong in faith
choose to abstain from what they know is acceptable
if their companions in Christ
find it objectionable.

Let us remember that we are all tempted
but not by the same things—
not to the same degree.
Let not the path we choose
be filled with pebbles of temptation for us
but that are boulders to others,
causing them to stumble and fall.

Let us not prize our liberties more highly
than the souls of our conservative sisters.
Let us consider how our actions
will affect other Christians.
Let us always strive to act in love
and not in self-indulgence.

Let us choose love over liberty
and be willing to relinquish our liberty—
forego a privilege—
for the sake of another.
Let us see the greater purpose—the higher calling
in showing love to another
than in doing what we love.
Let us not flaunt our freedom—
tempting those to sin
whom Christ died to set free
from the power of sin.

Body Building

We who are strong ought to bear with the failings of the weak and not to please ourselves. Each of us should please our neighbors for their good, to build them up. For even Christ did not please himself. (Romans 15:1–3)

The principal enemy of edification
is not animus toward our brothers
but selfishness.
For selfishness only seeks to please itself
and is always oblivious to the needs of others,
sometimes inadvertently hurting them.

We may not be tearing down our brothers,
but are we building them up?
We may not be pursuing conflict,
but are we working for peace?

God has made our faith strong,
so we can live intentionally—act purposefully
to build up our brothers and sisters in Christ.
Let us use that spiritual strength to help them
to fulfill their God-ordained potential—
to see their worth in God's family.

Let us build up our sisters
by pointing them to Christ,
not to ourselves—
by advising them with God's word
and not our words.

Let us be patient with our brothers
as God has been patient with us,
for building them up
is a process and not an event.
Let us realize
that if we live to please ourselves,
satisfaction becomes

- the treasure that can never found

- the race that can never be won

- the elusive dream that can never be grasped

Let us realize
that true joy is found
by living to please others for their good.
Let us discover
that fulfillment is achieved
by building up others for the glory of God.

Pray for One Another

> *I urge you, brothers and sisters, by our Lord Jesus Christ and by the love of the Spirit, to join me in my struggle by praying to God for me. (Romans 15:30)*

What can we do
when we cannot protect from danger
the ones we love?
Pray that God will protect them.
What can we do
when we have nothing to give for those in need?
Pray that God will provide.
What can we do
when those we love reject their Savior?
Pray that God will change their hearts.

Be diligent in praying for others.
Believe that God

- loves them more than we ever could

- can do more for them than we ever could

- will do what is best, not necessarily what we ask

Let us pray for others.
All of us need God's provision and protection.
All of us need his comfort and guidance.
No one glides through life untouched.
We all have hidden scars—unseen wounds.
Everyone suffers from the consequences of sin.
Everyone who seeks to do God's will
has suffered for the sake of Christ.

Let us never be so complacent, so uncaring,
that we fail to pray on behalf of others
who are facing struggles of their own.
Let us never be so ungrateful,
so forgetful of the grace we have received,
that we fail to pray for God's mercy
to fall on those in need.

Let us never place someone on such a high pedestal
that we think they do not need our prayers,
for all of us struggle—all are in need.
Let us never think so highly of ourselves—
be so filled with pride—
that we fail to ask others to pray for us.
For who does not need encouragement from others?
For who does not help from the Almighty?

Let us not allow anger and bitterness
to preclude our prayers
for those who have hurt us may need prayer the most.
Let us not stop praying
because we believe someone will never change,
for God did not give up on us
and will not give up on them.

As we pray to God on behalf of others,
those prayers change us.
Any thoughts of judgment
are transformed into prayers of mercy.
Any attitude of selfishness
become deep pools of compassion.
Any worries we have
are washed away by a desire to show kindness.

Alert to Danger

I urge you, brothers and sisters, to watch out for those who cause divisions and put obstacles in your way that are contrary to the teaching you have learned. Keep away from them. For such people are not serving our Lord Christ, but their own appetites. By smooth talk and flattery they deceive the minds of naive people. (Romans 16:17–18)

We know the world is a dangerous place,
but we expect the church to be a safe haven
where we can relax our guard

- assuming everything that is said is true

- trusting all the motives for what is done

But God has warned us to be alert.
Even within the church there are some
who cause divisions under the guise of unity—
who deceive for self-serving reasons.

These dividers and deceivers
put up obstacles contrary to God's word—
adding their own requirements and demands
to God's gracious gospel.
These dividers and deceivers
make promises that God has not made—
tempting us to follow them.

Spiritual deception is a plague.
But we can inoculate ourselves from its devastation
by absorbing truth from God's word.
Deception can be detected when we know God's word—
comparing it to the words of people
and rejecting anything not of God.

Spiritual division is a contagious disease
that can sweep throughout the church.
But we can isolate the disease
by not participating in divisive talk—
by not joining factions.

Remember that true spiritual leaders
point people to God and not to themselves.
True spiritual leaders
seek to unite the church in Christ and not divide it.

Remember that true spiritual leaders
put the needs of others ahead of their own interests.
True spiritual leaders
proclaim only God's truth and nothing else.

Section III:

The Goodness of God

A description of the sheer goodness of God has been woven through the fabric of the poems throughout the first two sections of *Gospel Psalms*. Section III brings the goodness of God into focus, as it examines certain characteristics and attributes of God. This is certainly not a comprehensive list but only includes those characteristics that are explicitly mentioned in the book of Romans.

As we come to see, understand, and experience the goodness of God, our hearts will respond. In general, we will want to thank God for all that he has done and to praise him for who he is. More specifically, as we

- understand the perfect righteousness of God, we find comfort that the all-powerful ruler of the universe always does what is right and just, and does not show favoritism;

- become aware of how merciful God has been to us, we are grateful that we did not receive the judgment we deserved but that God chose to spare us;

- experience the extravagant love of God, we are drawn to him and desire to love him in return;

- receive the abundant grace of God, we are humbled that God would do some much for someone so unworthy;

- learn of God's omniscience, we find peace and security, as we realize that everything and everyone has a purpose and place in God's plan;

- experience redemption by God, we rejoice in our freedom from the chains of sin, from the obligations of the law, and from the burden of guilt; and

- realize that God is the creator of all things, we are filled with hope, knowing that God will restore all things, eliminating the effects of sin.

Uncompromised Righteousness

> *God presented Christ as a sacrifice of atonement, through the shedding of his blood ... to demonstrate his righteousness, because in his forbearance he had left the sins committed beforehand unpunished—he did it to demonstrate his righteousness at the present time, so as to be just and the one who justifies those who have faith in Jesus (Romans 3:25–26)*

Even the best of us
make moral compromises—
have mixed motives.
Even the best of us
agonize about whether we should give others
the justice we know they deserve
or the grace our heart desires.
Even the best of us
sometimes sacrifice justice
at the altar of love.

But God is not that way.
His righteousness is never compromised.
God does not sacrifice justice
in order to demonstrate grace.
God does not abandon love
in order to be just.
God is able to be perfectly just and perfectly loving
at the same time.

Here is the wonder of God's gospel—
the glorious mystery of Christ's cross.
Through Christ's death,
both God's love and justice were satisfied.
God was not willing to allow all to perish in sin
because he loved us—
so God declared the unrighteous
to be righteous.

But God did not overlook our sins
to love us.
God did not waive sin's penalty
to demonstrate his grace.
God did not change divine law
to show us mercy.
God did not sacrifice justice
to demonstrate love.

On the cross
God's justice was satisfied once and for all.
He rendered punishment on Jesus
for our sins.
The penalty was paid in full
by the blood of Jesus,
for every sin—of every person—for all time.

Thanks to our God
for being the perfect judge.
We want justice, but we need mercy.
We are grateful that God is always just and fair
and yet always merciful and gracious.

Extravagant in Love

You see, at just the right time, when we were still powerless, Christ died for the ungodly. … But God demonstrates his own love for us in this: While we were still sinners, Christ died for us. (Romans 5:6, 8)

The gospel rests on a simple truth.

God loves us,

whoever we are, whatever we have done.

God's extravagant love is

- matchless in scope

- everlasting in duration

- selfless in nature

- independent of our response.

It is the extravagant love of God that

- draws us to him

- overcomes our fear

- overpowers our doubts

- persuades us to believe his promises

- inspires us to follow

The cross of Jesus Christ

tells us everything we need to know

about the extravagant love of God.

For God sent his only Son to that cross

- putting our sins on the sinless one

- punishing his Son for the sins we committed

- sacrificing Jesus's life for our lives

all so we could be reconciled to God.

Jesus willingly went to that cross,
enduring suffering and humiliation—
choosing to give up his life
so that we might be saved.
And the One who knew no sin
became sin
so that we—sinners by our very nature—
could be declared righteous in the sight of God.

There is no other love
like the extravagant love of God.
Who but God
would make the ultimate sacrifice
to save his enemies from the judgment they deserved?
Who but God
would give the costliest gift in all eternity
to those who had nothing to offer in return
except our animosity, our rebellion, our sin?

Thanks to our God,
who loves us more
than anyone else
ever would or ever could.
Thanks for God's outrageous love.
Anything less would not have been sufficient
to save our souls.

Abundant with Grace

> *Those who receive God's abundant provision of grace and of the gift of righteousness reign in life through the one man, Jesus Christ! ... where sin increased, grace increased all the more. (Romans 5:17, 20)*

The abundant grace of God is
freely offered and freely given,
overflowing from God's reservoirs—
pouring over the earth
to all who trust in him.

Praise God for the wonder of his grace—
for as our sins increased, so did God's grace.
No matter how dark our sins became,
God's light was brighter.

No matter how grievous our sins,
God's forgiveness was greater.
No matter how numerous our sins,
God's grace covered them all.

The abundant grace of God
provides all we need.
By his grace,
the unrighteous are given righteousness—
the spiritually dead are given eternal life.
By his grace,
those suffering are given comfort
and sinners receive forgiveness.

By God's grace,
the undeserving are given
what they do not deserve.
The unworthy receive
what they do not merit.
Who but God
would give righteousness to the unrighteous—
would forgive the sinner of his sins?
Who but God
would freely give
that which cost him so much?

Thanks to our Lord,
who chose to grant us his favor,
for lavishing us with his grace,
layer upon layer—filling our gaps
with his perfection.

Power-Filled Love

> *For I am convinced that neither death nor life, neither angels*
> *nor demons, neither the present nor the future, nor any powers,*
> *neither height nor depth, nor anything else in all creation, will*
> *be able to separate us from the love of God that is in Christ Jesus*
> *our Lord. (Romans 8:38-39)*

In the human condition,

power without love

is ruthlessly self-centered—

exclusively self-serving.

Power not bridled by love,

knows no boundaries, and has no restraints.

In the human condition,

love without power

is an impotent emotion—

unable to help and protect the objects of its affection.

But God is not like us.

His character is the perfect union

between unconditional love and unlimited power.

The unconditional love of God is propelled by his power.

The absolute power of God is directed by his love.

God's love is power-filled.

God's power is love-infused.

That is why

nothing can separate us from the love of God.

We thank the Lord
that his power-filled love will always protect us.
There is

- no distance too great

- no future so uncertain

- no opposition too strong

God's love never grows weary—
never runs dry.

We are grateful to the Lord
that his power-filled love cannot be limited.
There is

- no one so unworthy

- no one so sinful

- no one so rebellious

to be beyond the reach of his love.

In God is the perfect harmony of power and love.
His love never falters—never flickers.
It continually binds us with him.
His fiercely protective love is able
to guard our salvation against all threats—all powers.
For the lover of our souls
is the ruler of the universe

He is

- the victor over death

- the giver of life

- the author and finisher of our salvation

It is a love we may never comprehend
but a love we can always trust.
It is a love from the heart of God
that touched our hearts
and transformed our souls.

Thanks to our Lord
who is always able—always willing—
to love us.

Love Not Like Ours

> *God's love has been poured out into our hearts through the Holy Spirit. (Romans 5:5)*

Our circle of love is often small

- our family and friends

- those easily loveable

- those who love in return

But the expansive love of God is matchless

- broad enough to extend to his enemies

- deep enough to reach the worst sinner

- strong enough to penetrate the hardest heart

Our love is fragile—
easily broken by adversity,
quickly diminished by rejection.
But the love of God is
unbreakable, unstoppable, everlasting,
cascading over his people in an unending flow.

Too often we give love

only because we want to receive love in return.

Too often we show love

only because we need to be loved—

blending affection with selfishness.

But the love of God is not like ours.

God does not need to receive love

in order to give love.

He is the source of love—the initiator of love.

The love of God is unconditional,

for it does not depend on our goodness—

does not wait for our response

but continues to pour over us.

And it is that lavish love

that causes us to love God.

Sovereign in Mercy

I will have mercy on whom I have mercy, and I will have compassion on whom I have compassion." It does not, therefore, depend on human desire or effort, but on God's mercy … Therefore God has mercy on whom he wants to have mercy, and he hardens whom he wants to harden. (Romans 9:15–16, 18)

Everyone deserves to receive God's wrath,
for all have sinned against him.
No one deserves to receive his mercy,
for none are worthy.
God has no obligation to give mercy,
and we have no right to demand it.

Some will receive the mercy
they do not deserve.
Others will receive the wrath
they have earned.
God alone determines
who will receive mercy
and who will receive judgment.

The Lord God is high and lifted up!
Only God would show such compassion
that cost him so much.
Only God would save his enemies
from the judgment they deserve.
Only God would give mercy
to those who have rebelled against him.

God's sovereign mercy allows no room for boasting—
no place for our pride.
For the beneficiaries of his mercy
are not those who worked harder to please him,
are not those whose character was better,
but are simply those chosen by God to be spared.

As we understand the depth and darkness of our sin,
We see the fullness of God's grace.
As we realize we have been spared from hell,
we see the richness of his mercy.

Let us toss aside our pride and walk in humility
and praise God from a heart of gratitude.
Let us pray for others to be recipients of God's mercy
and not objects of his wrath.

Only God is worthy to decide
who receives mercy, who receives judgment,
for he alone is perfect in holiness,
absolute in sovereignty, full of compassion.
We rejoice that God decides our eternal destiny

Incomprehensible Omniscience

Oh, the depth of the riches of the wisdom and knowledge of God! How unsearchable his judgments, and his paths beyond tracing out! "Who has known the mind of the Lord? Or who has been his counselor. (Romans 11:33–34)

No matter how wise we know God to be,
he is wiser than that.
The finite can never fully comprehend
the thoughts of the infinite.
The temporal can never understand
the ways of the eternal.

There is nothing we can say
that God does not already know.
None of us knows what tomorrow will bring,
yet God knows the future for a thousand generations.

The Lord is perfect in wisdom.
He knows how all things came to be,
for He created everything from nothing.
God knows how all things will end
because he has ordained the future.

With God there are no mistakes—
no unintended consequences, no delays.
His purposes are always accomplished
just the way he intended—
at just the right time.

With God there are no random occurrences—
no chance encounters.
Everything has a part in God's purpose—
has a place in his plan.

There is much we do not understand about God,
much we will never be able to comprehend.
But failing to understand
does not diminish our faith—does not shake our trust.

What God has revealed to us
has always proven to be true.
What we have experienced from God
has always been compassionate.
What we have witnessed of his actions
has always been righteous.
We know enough to praise him.
We know enough to trust him.

Redeemer

> *And all are justified freely by his grace through the redemption*
> *that came by Christ Jesus. (Romans 3:24)*

We had incurred a penalty for our sin

that we could not pay

but God redeemed us.

Jesus paid the penalty on our behalf,

taking the punishment that we deserved,

giving his life in exchange for our life.

We were enslaved by sin.

There was no escape from its allure.

But God redeemed us—cutting the chains that held us,

freeing us from the power of sin

with the victorious resurrection of Jesus

We were under the requirements of the law,

obligated to meet all its standards

but failing to keep them.

But Jesus redeemed us,

fulfilling the law on our behalf

with his perfect, sinless life.

We were under the burden of guilt

for the sins we had committed,

carrying the weight of our transgressions,

But Jesus redeemed us.

Thank you, Jesus,

for lifting that burden with your forgiveness—

healing our wounds with your blood.

Creator-Sustainer

For from him and through him and for him are all things.
(Romans 11:36)

God is the creator of all things.
Nothing exists except what God has made.
Everything we know
was created by him.
Everything we are yet to discover
was created by him.

As we look further and further into space,
we see
the hand of the Creator—the mind of the Designer—
everywhere we look.
The planets, stars, and galaxies
all dance to the master's music in perfect harmony.

As we looker deeper and deeper in the subatomic world,
we see
the hand of the Creator—the mind of the Designer—
everywhere we look.
Protons, neutrons, and quarks
are God's invisible glue
that holds the universe together.

The infinitely large and the infinitely small
are all conceived by the mind of the Creator.
The infinitely large and the infinitely small
are all made by the hands of the Creator.
As we look closer and closer into the mirror,
we see
the hand of the Creator—the mind of the Designer.
We were

- created by God in his image

- given life by the very breath of God

- delegated to rule the earth on his behalf

- intended to live with God forever

But we rebelled against our Creator,
introducing sin, death, and decay into creation.
The image of God within us has been

- marred by the graffiti of sin

- broken by the vandalism of our transgressions

- blackened by the flames of our rebellion

But God's plans are never thwarted—
his purposes are always accomplished.
What seems a detour, a deviation, or a defeat
is all part of his grand design.

God has reconciled sinful people to himself,
making us his holy people
so we can live with him forever,
just as God intended.
God has redeemed a rebellious people
so we can rule the earth for God,
just as he planned.

God will make a new heaven and new earth,
wiping away the stench of sin
we introduced into his good creation.
God will restore all things.

The age of sin
will be but a blip on eternity's screen—
a blink of the eyes of the infinite.
Once again God will say,
It is good.
And once again,
all creation will give glory to God,
forever and forever.

Glory to God

To him be the glory forever! Amen. (Romans 11:36)

We were trash
headed to the incinerator.
But God pulled us from the dumpster,
recycling us, repurposing our lives,
making what had been worthless
now treasured.

We were rebellious children
willfully wandering away
until we were hopelessly lost,
but God relentlessly searched
until he found us and brought us back home.

We were inmates on death row,
guilty as charged,
waiting for the inevitable.
But God intervened,
acquitting the guilty,
giving new life to those destined to die.

We were drowning in the sea of sin,
futilely trying to save ourselves,
but God rescued us,
pulling us into his life raft
just as we were going under
for the last time.

We were children of the streets,
homeless, fatherless, penniless.
We were unwanted, unworthy, unloved.
But God saw society's outcasts
hiding in plain sight
and adopted us into his family,
showering us with his love.

All glory to God,
for he is worthy.
All praise to God,
for he is good.

Made in the USA
Middletown, DE
30 September 2017